"Lightning in a Bottle is a
Dr. Mike Palompo guides .... .c people
God designed us to be. The Temple is more than a historical lay-out of an ancient tradition. It is a blueprint, a
map, a plan that God intentionally ordained to lead us
back to the Holy of Holies when we have lost our way."

Dr. Wayne Cordeiro
Founder and President - New Hope International
(a network of 138 churches and ministries)
Author of *Doing Church As Team, Divine Mentor,*
and a dozen other titles

"From the beginning, God has taught his people that life
with him is a progressive journey, and he has given us
numerous lessons to keep us on track. In his book,
Lightning in a Bottle, Mike Palompo explores the way in
which the ancient Temple in Jerusalem was itself a God-
given symbolic template for the spiritual progress of the
individual. With characteristic insight, energy and wit,
Mike leads us through the elements of the Temple's
design, and we see them as stations on a path of development in the presence of God. This book is a powerful
meditation on a timeless symbol, made wonderfully
practical with reflections and well-conceived discussion
questions. It's perfect for small group studies or personal devotions. It's a brilliant tool for deepening and
progress."

Dr. Jordan Seng
Senior Pastor, Bluewater Mission, Honolulu, HI
Author of *Miracle Work: A Down-to-Earth Guide for
Supernatural Ministries*

"Pastor Michael Palompo is a man of integrity; someone
who wisely watches over what God has entrusted to
him. He has a passion for true transformation. His work
incorporates the Hebraic foundations and understand-

ing of the original biblical texts. By focusing on the seven key implements in the Tabernacle, called in Hebrew Mishkan, Pastor Palompo unveils the foreshadowing of Messiah and God's perfect plan of redemption. *Lightning in a Bottle* is a very timely and truly life-changing book. This is a call to love Adonai with all our heart, mind, soul and being."

Yamit McCormick
Instructor of Biblical Hebrew Language and Culture
Pacific Rim Christian University, Honolulu, HI

"For the last 40 years I've watched Jesus continue His amazing work in Mike Palompo. I was there the night he put his faith in Jesus Christ and I continue to see the same passion and excitement exhibited in his life. *Lightning in a Bottle* is filled with lessons learned from a man who loves God and has lived out the truths that he describes. His creative and honest style will challenge you to revisit the power of the transforming Spirit in your own life and the Bible's claim that you are truly the temple of the Holy Spirit. The living God dwells in you!"

Pastor Mark Olmos, D.Min. in progress
Discipleship Pastor, Palm Valley Church, Goodyear, AZ

Lightning in a Bottle

Our Odyssey to Temple the Holy Spirit

Michael M. Palompo, D.Min.

Also by Michael M. Palompo

God Things
Encounters with Jesus that Transform Us

ISBN-13: 978-1512071412
ISBN-10: 1512071412

Cover Design by Mark Palompo

To Mark Andrew Palompo
Jalee Kate Palompo
Rachael Elizabeth Mie Palompo
Caleb Michael Palompo
Beloved children, arrows in our quiver,
& Temples of the Holy Spirit

Table of Contents

PROLOGUE
    Preface - 15
    Introduction - 21
    Overview: The Temple Template - 31
        Thesis of *Lightning in a Bottle* - 33
        Diagram: The Temple Template - 34
    Praxis - 53
        The Mind of Christ - 69
    Prayer in the Temple Courts - 77

PART 1　The Outer Court: CONNECT - 87
    Chapter 1　The Bronze Altar: *Salvation* - 93
    Chapter 2　The Bronze Basin: *Sanctification* - 103

PART 2　The Holy Place: EQUIP - 113
    Chapter 3　The Golden Table of Bread:
        Scripture - 119
    Chapter 4　The Golden Lamp:
        Testimony - 131
        From Filipino Playboy to Man of God - 143
    Chapter 5　The Golden Altar of Incense:
        Prayer - 151

PART 3　The Holy of Holies:
    TRANSFORM - 163
    Chapter 6　The Ark of the Covenant:
        Spiritual Leadership - 171
        The Ten Commandments - 175
        The Jar of Manna - 181
        The Staff of Aaron - 185
    Chapter 7　The Mercy Seat:
        Great Commission - 193

EPILOGUE

Aftermath - 213

APPENDICES

Appendix A: Transformation Academy - 221
Appendix B: Personal Inventory - 235
Appendix C: Shema` Family Discipleship - 241

About the Author - 251
Acknowledgements - 253

Prologue

Preface

"If I had asked people what they wanted,
they would have said faster horses."
Henry Ford

Why write *Lightning in a Bottle*?   As I observe the church, I have noticed that there is an upper case "C" *Church* and a lower case "c" *church*.   The *Church* has Jesus at the center and does *God Things.*[1] Whereas the *church* has man at the center and does good things.

In the *Church* there is a declaration that Jesus is the Head. He is invited to lead at all gatherings—Sunday services, board meetings, staff meetings, small group meetings, youth meetings, etc.

It is not bound to any particular organizational structure or form. There may still be liturgy, tradition, and program, but it is more organism than organization. There is often a strong sense of His Presence. Everyone is inclined to listen to what the Spirit is saying. Personal agendas are set aside in order to arrive by faith at how the Spirit is leading. The *Church* is intentional about doing God Things (what God is actually doing) rather than good things (things done in the name of God but have little to do with God).

By contrast, in the *church* there is only a traditional opening prayer. And then people take over with their agendas. The *church* is more organization than organism. God is not invited to lead at the gatherings. Jesus accomplished His work over 2,000 years ago or during some previous awakening. There is no anticipation He would do anything today. So it is all up to us now to make something happen. People are focused on other people—especially the pastor. Did he give a good sermon? Was he funny? Is he "anointed?" Did I feel "fed" after his message? The focus is on the *personality* of the pastor rather than the *Person* of Jesus. The *church* does a lot of ministry but fails to do God's will—many good things, little or no *God Things*.

What is the difference between church and Church? ___

_____

The reality is that the *Church* probably exists within many local congregations, and it is not so cut and dry. I'm being stark to make a point. I have noticed that without focus and intentionality, *Church* becomes *church* in a heartbeat. We often begin with a strong sense of leading and calling, but then slip very easily into program and routine. We begin with a powerful move of God and wind up with a hollow shell of our former selves. We have buildings with no Spiritual life—plenty of money but no heart. The movement has become a monument.

How do we remain the *Church*—full of Spiritual vitality and power? How do we regain our focus and find our way back...and forward? *Church* is supposed to be about God but how do we stop it from becoming about something else? How do we stop this from happening? I believe there is a way.

I like how the Apostles did *Church* in the book of Acts—the Spirit prompting, the Spirit speaking, the Spirit leading, and everyone filled with awe. Stunning! I don't like the *church* at Laodicea (Rev. 3:20): Jesus is standing outside of *church*, knocking on the door, hoping to be invited in! Stunned.

Years ago I was talking with a friend who was about to plant a *church*. He said he was given a kit with all the tools he would need to start a *church*. Imagine that. A do-it-yourself tool kit for doing *church—church* in a box. I can actually see how such a box would be useful (how to incorporate your church, sample bylaws, organizational structures, which teams to build first, etc.). But the thought of *reducing* the *Church* to that blew my mind. And I am certain my friend would never knowingly reduce the *Church* to that. There is so much more to us than being a business or a social agency.

In a related subject, atheists began having *church* in 2013. They call it the "Sunday Assembly," and they claim it is a growing phenomenon. "Atheist *church*." Now there's an oxymoron for you—like "jumbo shrimp," "government intelligence," or "Microsoft Works." (Just kidding, Bill Gates, I have both a Mac and a PC.) The atheist *church* has all the trappings of *church*—singing, fellowship, even a sermon—but no God. It is a godless *church*.

If you listen to their "testimonies" on YouTube, many members of atheist *church* used to go to a Christian *church*. They felt judged and condemned so they left. They blamed God for that. But it sounds to me like they were already attending a godless *church*. They merely traded a Christian godless *church* for an atheist one.

Why did atheists start doing church in 2013? _____

_____

What does that say to you about the difference between church and Church? _____

_____

The problem with a *church* that appeals to what people think they need is that people do not really know what they need. Henry Ford once said, "If I had asked people what they wanted, they would have said faster horses." Who knows best what people really need? God does. He created human beings. He knows us better than we know ourselves. Instead of asking people what they need, let's find out God's vision for us.

So why write *Lightning in a Bottle*? My prayer is that we have a conversation about what it means to be the *Church* instead of the *church*. How do we go from being a human-driven organization to a Spirit-led organism? How do we embrace the reality that God's vision for us is better than our vision for ourselves?

God's vision for us is to become the location of His Presence on the Earth.

Let me be quick to add that the fellowship I lead, New Hope Central Oahu, has a long way to go in this area. My heart is to sit in the classroom with Professor Jesus co-learning with you. This book is me turning in a single term paper on our subject. This is only the beginning of a lifelong conversation.

Remember the key difference between *Church* and *church*. In a *church* Jesus is outside hoping to be invited in. In a *Church* He is inside leading the way. *Lightning in a Bottle* is about *Church* not *church*. Sometimes our focus is on becoming a *church* that people want to go to. But are we a *Church* that God would want to come to?

How do we become a Church that God would want to come to? _____

_____

Summarize why you think Mike wrote this book. _____

_____

As you study *Lightning in a Bottle,* by faith what do you believe the Holy Spirit wants to teach you? _____

_____

_____

1. See *God Things: Encounters with Jesus that Transform Us*, available on Amazon and Kindle.

19

Introduction

Temples Then, Now, and Future

Judging from what happened in Laodicea, Jesus wants to be invited to transform *church* into *Church*. As you continue reading, pray and invite Him to show you how He does that very thing these days:

"Lord, I throw the door of my heart wide open for You to come and lead me on my odyssey to temple Your Presence on Earth."

Let's go all the way back to the beginning. We get the word "tabernacle" or "temple" from the Hebrew root word *mishkan,* which means "sanctuary" or simply "tent." Here's the passage:

"Have them make a sanctuary for me and I will dwell among them" (Exodus 25:8 NIV).

In this verse the word for "sanctuary" is *mikdash.* The Hebrew word for "and I will dwell" is *veshakhanti.* So in Hebrew the verse reads like this: "Have them make a *mikdash veshakhanti* with them." Both *mikdash and veshakhanti* come from the same Hebrew root word *mishkan.* Therefore, the purpose of the *mishkan* was to be a dwelling where God would tabernacle, or "pitch His tent," right next to everybody else's. Isn't that amazing?

The *Mishkan* Temple is where God and man live.

Summarize in your own words God's heart and purpose for the *Mishkan* Temple. _____

_____

Throughout the Bible the representation of the Presence of God with His people kept evolving as God revealed His plan to mankind. What were these representations?

As we just saw, in the Old Testament God's Presence with His people centered on the Tabernacle (while they were nomads) and later the Temple (when they settled in Jerusalem).

In the New Testament God's Presence with us centered on the Person of Jesus Christ. "And the Word became flesh and dwelt among us" (John 1:14 NASB). Jesus referred to Himself as the *Mishkan* Temple (John 2:19).

Jesus is absolutely critical for us to live in the Presence of God. He is the very Presence of God with us in human form. And as we shall see later, He provides the only Way for us to be with God.

But where is God's Presence with us today?

Today the physical body of the Lord Jesus no longer walks the Earth. No one has seen a man with a robe, sandals, and beard who looks like Jim Caviezel. The Bible tells us Jesus ascended into Heaven and sits at the right hand of the Father. His *body* is in a glorified state in a timeless dimension, i.e. Heaven.

So according to the Bible where is the Presence of God today? Some will say, "He's everywhere." That, of course, is not incorrect. God is omnipresent. He is in Heaven. He is on Earth. He is in the universe. He is beyond the universe.

But although He is present everywhere, He is not always *manifest* everywhere. His presence everywhere remains invisible. The Tabernacle was a place where a manifestation or re-presentation of God's presence could occur. God encounters happened in the *Mishkan*. The bible talks about how fire came forth from the Tabernacle (Lev. 9:24).

Jesus was the perfect physical manifestation of the Father. "The Son is the radiance of God's glory and the exact representation of His being" (Heb. 1:3a NIV). "No one has ever seen God, but the one and only Son, who is himself God and is in closest relationship with the Father, has made him known" (John 1:18 NIV).

So let me ask the question more clearly: "Where is the physical manifestation of God-with-us *on the Earth* today?"

The Bible says your body is the Temple of the Holy Spirit.

The Presence of God on Earth today is within His Church.

"Do you not know that you are a temple of God and that the Holy Spirit dwells in you" (1 Corinthians 3:16

NASB)?

"Your body is a temple of the Holy Spirit" (1 Corinthians 6:19 NASB).

Paul did not say the Church *is* God. He said the Spirit of God exists within the members of the Christian Church. The Holy Spirit dwells in the Church body *corporately*. The Holy Spirit dwells in the body of each Christian *individually*. So when we are in Church together, the Holy Spirit is in us. When you are home alone the Spirit is still in you. If you are a genuine Christian, the Presence of God exists within you.

The Creator of the universe lives inside you.

Summarize the progression of God's *Mishkan* Presence with us on the Earth from the Old Testament to today. __

I don't know about you, but as I reflect on that reality—the Creator of the universe living inside me—I'm like, "Whaaat?" There's just no way for me to fully wrap my head around that. It breaches the limits of credulity. The concept is just too farfetched for my mortal mind to comprehend much less accept. Anyone else besides me feel this way? I'm just not "comfortable" with that thought.

In fact, it is so beyond us, most Christians I know live in a kind of denial about it. They cannot deny that the Bible says it, so they're like, "Oh yes, I have accepted Jesus in my heart." But I'm like, "Do you have any idea what you just said? You're saying the God who created the universe—we're talking about a gazillion stars, countless planets, galaxy after galaxy, not to mention every grain of sand, every molecule, every atom, across dimensions you or I could not possibly fathom—THAT God...lives in your heart." HOW IS THAT EVEN POSSI-BLE? The fact that we say that with such a cavalier, nonchalant attitude betrays the truth that we really don't get it.

The other attitude I see reduces the notion to the need for Christians to get in better shape. "Our body is a temple," so we need to exercise and eat healthy. While this is a worthy issue for the Church to tackle (how many obese pastors do you know?), it is beyond the scope of this book.

When I come to passages like 1 Corinthians 3:16 and 6:19, the best approach is not to dilute what the Scrip-tures say so I can be more "comfortable" with it. My comfort is not the goal. Rather, I want my life to come into alignment with what God says. This should make us *uncomfortable*.

Listen, sending Jesus to die for our sin was never *our* idea. This was all God's doing. We get to be the recipi-ents of His amazing grace. In the same way, Pentecost was not *our* idea. It was not *our* idea for God to baptize us with His Spirit and inhabit our bodies. Once again we just get to be the recipients.

So when God does these outlandish, fantastic things, our place is to simply humble ourselves and maybe say, "Wow, Lord, I would not have done it this way. I would have chosen someone else. But ok, let Your will be done in my life." And of course, "Thank you, beyond what words can express."

Mother Mary is an excellent example of someone who finds herself in this situation. The Angel Gabriel tells her she is to bear a son who will be the Messiah of the world—the Immanuel that Isaiah prophesied. Mary's what, maybe seventeen? She is a virgin. She is unmarried. She is willing to do God's will, but she immediately confesses she has no clue how. I can totally relate. Like Mother Mary we say, "Behold the handmaiden of the Lord."

Today we find ourselves in a similar predicament as Mary. This book is about stepping out in faith to be a living, breathing temple of the Holy Spirit—the *Mishkan* Presence of God on the Earth today. It is about taking God at His word. Making us hosts of His Presence was *His* choice not ours. It is about humbly embracing God's vision for us and setting aside whatever vision we may have had for ourselves. It is about pressing through whatever discomfort, incredulity, misgivings, skepticism, or frankly, unbelief we may be feeling in order to become fully surrendered and—here it is—*obedient* to His will for us. We pray one of my oft-spoken prayers, "Lord, help me in my unbelief."

Too often Church focuses on getting people to Heaven not getting Heaven into the people.

Share your heart on how you feel about becoming the *Mishkan* Presence of God on Earth. _____

_____

It does sound too good to be true, but this is how God feels about us—how deeply He loves us. And deep down in our hearts this is what every child of God truly longs for. "The one thing I ask of the Lord—the thing I seek most—is to live in the house of the Lord all the days of my life, delighting in the Lord's perfections and meditating in his Temple" (Psalm 27:4 NLT).

So what is the inevitable future that mankind is hurtling toward? What awaits those who overcome?

Actually, in the future there will be no Temple. Do you know why? John the Apostle reveals: "I saw no Temple in the city, for the Lord God Omnipotent [Himself] and the Lamb [Himself] are its Temple" (Revelation 21:22 AMP).

Remember, the whole purpose of the Temple is to have a place where God and man live in harmony. In the New Heaven and New Earth, God Himself becomes the Temple. There won't be a Temple (stone or human) because we won't need one. God will be visible to us everywhere for all eternity.

In a way beyond our imagining the physical and spiritual dimensions merge into one. The metaphysical veil that prevents us from seeing the supernatural dimension will be gone. We will have transformed into beings patterned after the resurrected body of Jesus.

The future is all about dwelling in God's awesome Presence for all eternity. Our vision for our Christian lives must prepare us for this reality. Church needs to understand this vision then establish a strategy and a culture that helps people understand and fulfill the vision.

If you share this vision, then *Lightning in a Bottle* was written for you.

In light of what you now know about God's future vision for Heaven and Earth, what do you need to learn? _____

_____

A *denominative* is a verb we create that comes from a noun. The word literally means "from a noun." For example "milk" is a thing not an action. But we can turn it into an action: "Milk the cow." When you think about it, we do this all the time. "*Bridge* the gap." "*Text* me." "I was *floored* when I heard the news." "*Hand* over the gun." "*Book 'em*, Dano." The word "temple" is typically a noun. But in this book I will at times use it as a verb—a denominative. We *temple* the Holy Spirit.

The Holy Spirit, the very presence of God, lives within disciples of Jesus. God is not just a billion miles away somewhere in the universe or beyond it. And He's not just in Heaven. God is as close to us as the air in our lungs, as the blood in our veins. His thoughts can be our thoughts. The very bodies of the faithful are the new temples of the Holy Spirit.

We can have a life beyond the mundane. Join me in this quest of a lifetime! From the moment we were born we knew there was something more to life and more to *us* than meets the eye. Let's go on a journey toward the more. Become *lightning in a bottle* and begin your odyssey to *temple the Holy Spirit.*

By faith what did the Holy Spirit say to you in this section? How will you obey Him? _____

_____

Overview
The Temple Template

You bring the ordinary; God brings the extra.
That makes you extraordinary!
You bring the natural; God brings the super.
That makes you supernatural!
You bring the bottle; God brings the lightning.
And you become lightning in a bottle!

You are the Temple of the Holy Spirit. The reason we want to study the Temple in Jerusalem is to understand how God designed us to be the Temple of the Holy Spirit. The better we understand the Temple, the better we understand ourselves.

The layout of the *Mishkan* was a revelation from God Himself. God was very specific and intentional about its design. Each room, each piece of furniture had profound significance. Here were God's precise instructions:

"Make this tabernacle and all its furnishings *exactly* (italics mine) like the pattern I will show you" (Exodus 25:9 NIV).

We need to ask, "Lord, why did you set up the Tabernacle *exactly* the way You did?" First, we need to know that the lessons are virtually inexhaustible. And it is not my intent in this book to give an exhaustive teaching. Fundamentally, however, you should know this:

The earthly Mishkan was a "copy and shadow of what is in Heaven" (Hebrews 8:5 NASB). I like the word *hardcopy*.

The Temple on Earth is a hardcopy of the Temple in Heaven. Amazing and glorious things are happening in the heavenly courts. The earthly Temple is a hardcopy of what is going on in the Spirit. God is doing awesome things in the *actual* Temple in the heavenly realm.

How do we in the natural realm comprehend what is happening in the supernatural? Look at the hardcopy! By following our hardcopy we will better understand the Person and mission of Jesus. Our hardcopy holds the keys to unlocking the mysteries of how *we* temple the Spirit.

We will focus on seven key *stations* in the *Mishkan* represented by a significant piece of furnishing: the Bronze Altar, the Bronze Basin, the Golden Table of Bread, the Golden Lamp, the Golden Altar of Incense, the Ark of the Covenant, and the Mercy Seat.

I call them *stations* rather than *steps* to avoid the suggestion that the process has to be perfectly linear. During our lifetime odyssey to intimacy with God, the Spirit of Truth will highlight what He wants to teach us in the season we're in. Sometimes He might return us to a station to re-teach or expand on a lesson. Our journey may not be a straight line from A to Z, but that doesn't mean that God didn't have a process in mind. We should pay attention to the progression as we journey toward the deepest place of intimacy with God. Remember God designed the Temple. There is a logical and intentional sequence to our odyssey.

Remember the principle of "Order of Operations" from math class? What is 2+2x3? There is only one correct answer to this problem. But is it 12 or 8? To solve this problem correctly we must use the order of operations. Multiplication comes before addition. So we multiply 2x3 first, then add 2. The answer is 8.

In the same way there is an order of operations in our odyssey to the deepest place of intimacy with God. If we skip a station or didn't learn its lesson well, something inevitably goes wrong. So since God told Moses to build the Tabernacle exactly according to His specifications, we will follow God's order of operations.

Thesis of *Lightning in a Bottle*

Therefore, by understanding God's design of the Temple as His way of taking us on an odyssey to *connect*, *equip*, and *transform*, we grow in our intimacy with the person and mission of Jesus and discover how we too might *temple the Spirit.*

Summarize the thesis of this book and the relationship between the Temple, Jesus, and us. _____

_____

The Temple Template

W

Mercy Seat

Ark of the Covenant

HOLY OF HOLIES

Golden Altar of Incense

S

Golden Lamp

Golden Table of Bread

N

HOLY PLACE

Bronze Basin

Bronze Altar

OUTER COURT

E

The Temple Template

A *template* is a pattern or guide we follow in order to copy an original. Did you know the word "template" is derived from the 17th century English word "templet" which very likely came from "temple?" The Temple is our template for how to temple His Spirit.

God's ultimate plan was never to provide a blueprint for how to build a stone temple but rather to show us how we temple His Spirit.

What follows is a summary of the blueprint of the *Mishkan* and how it relates to Jesus and us. The *Mishkan* holds the key to how God intended for us to encounter Him. Within the design of the *Mishkan*, God shows us how we access Him, and how this was fulfilled in Christ Jesus. The *Mishkan* Temple is a foreshadowing of you. The Holy Spirit is the Presence of Jesus within you.

Let us begin.

The Temple was where priests would minister to one another and to the Lord. Today, Christians are the "royal priesthood" (1 Peter 2:9).

The priests would approach from the east side and proceed westward. We begin outside, journey inward, then re-engage the outside world in a powerful way. We first experience *connection*, then *equipping*, and finally *transformation*.

CONNECT

Before we enter the actual *Mishkan* Temple the priests would be standing in the Outer Court. Two key stations are found here: (1) The Bronze Altar, (2) The Bronze

Basin.

The Bronze Altar: Salvation

The Bronze Altar was where animal sacrifices were made for the atonement of sin. It is a traumatic experience to see an animal slaughtered, especially when you find out it was killed because of our sin. The bloody and deadly consequence of sin is played out before us in living color. But it was much more than that. It was also God's plan to redeem us.

> **The people of God learned
> very early on that an innocent
> could die in place of the guilty.**

This foreshadowed the ultimate substitutionary sacrifice for the sin of mankind—the Crucifixion of Jesus. We receive by faith the amazing grace of God, a full pardon for our sin through the finished work of Jesus on the cross. This is salvation! This is what the bible means by being born again.

And so our odyssey begins: not by religious effort on our part, and never because we made ourselves righteous, but rather by the love and grace of God.

By accepting Jesus, we are accepted before we are acceptable. We are perfectly loved before becoming perfectly lovable. We *connect* with Jesus.

There is a "Bronze Altar" within you. Have you received Christ into your life for the forgiveness of your sin? If not, simply come to Jesus right now and pray this prayer from your heart:

"Heavenly Father, thank you for Jesus. Jesus, thank you for dying for my sin on the cross. I confess that I have sinned, and I repent from living for myself. I receive your forgiveness for my sin as a free gift. Baptize me with Your Spirit and I will follow You all the rest of my days. In Jesus' Name, Amen."

Summarize the Bronze Altar and its relationship between the Temple, Jesus, and you. _____

_____

The Bronze Basin: Sanctification

Once we have put our faith in Jesus, He leads us now from the Bronze Altar to the Bronze Basin. This is where the priests would ritually wash with the water in the basin. It was a place of sanctification. We become holy as God is holy.

Now that we belong to Jesus, He purifies us.

> **We came to Jesus *just as we are,***
> **but He loves us too much**
> **to leave us *just as we are.***

He means to draw us into a closer and closer relationship with Him. We can't do that if we have issues. Now by the cleansing streams of the Holy Spirit, we are being set free from the hold that sin has on us. Through the cross we were set free from the *penalty* of sin; now we are being set free from sin's *power*.

There is a Bronze Basin within us where the Spirit must set us free. A stronghold is anything that has a "strong hold" on us. Strongholds must be identified and broken by the power of the Spirit. Because of His zeal for the

Temple, Jesus threw out the moneychangers and over-turned their tables. He is just as zealous to transform our temple from a "den of thieves" to a "house of prayer." He is breaking us free from the world to set us apart—consecrate us—to Himself. At the Bronze Basin He leads us to leave behind worldly ways before enter-ing His Temple.

Summarize the Bronze Basin and its relationship be-tween the Temple, the Spirit, and you. _____

_____

From *connection* in the Outer Court we are then *equipped* in the Holy Place.

EQUIP

Making a decision for Christ is far and away the most important decision in a person's life. We can go no further in our odyssey to God's Manifest Presence un-less we connect with Jesus. What happens next needs to be carefully understood. Once we are saved we now have access to God as His gift to us. If we were to die right now we would have eternal life in Heaven by the grace of God. However, how many of us know that there is so much more to salvation than a free ticket to Heaven?

Many Christians, while waiting to go to Heaven, fail to experience the fullness of the Presence of God-with-us on Earth.

Have you ever felt like there must be more to a relation-ship with God than what you are experiencing? The Temple is our template for how to temple the Spirit.

Now that we've received Christ and are being cleansed by His Spirit, He leads us from the Outer Court to inside the Tabernacle. We are no longer outside. We are now inside a room about the size of a large living room. This room is called the "Holy Place."

Remember that Jesus is the Temple. So when we enter the Holy Place we are now *in* Christ. This is where the priests gathered for fellowship. It is a place of *equipping*.

Within the Holy Place on the right side of the room (north) is the Golden Table of Bread. On the left side (south) is the Golden Lamp with seven lights. Directly in front of us (west) in the center toward the back is the Golden Altar of Incense.

The Golden Table of Bread: Scripture

The table highlights the importance of *fellowship* with one another. But this is not just socializing for fun. The bread is the Bread of His Presence. Jesus is the Bread of Life. We gather around Him at the center. Now this is fun with deep significance!

When tempted in the wilderness to turn stones into bread, Jesus said, "Man shall not live on bread alone, but on every word that comes from the mouth of God" (Matthew 4:4 NIV cf. Deuteronomy 8:3).

**The Bread that we need for our existence
is the Living Word, not a stale,
merely academic exercise in the Bible.**

In fellowship there needs to be a strong emphasis on the Living Word of God. Each of us is designed with a special table in our hearts where we flourish in fellowship with others as we share in the Bread of His Living Word.

Summarize the Golden Table of Bread and its relationship between the Temple, Jesus, and you. _____

The Golden Lamp: Testimony

The Golden Lamp, or candelabrum, is also called the Menorah. In the book of Revelation this lampstand represents the Church. The light from the Golden Lamp is the Light of Christ. This station teaches us the importance of *testimony*.

Jesus, the Light of the world (John 8:12; 9:5), says to the Church, "You are the light of the world" (Matthew 5:14). Christians are the light of the world. Each of us is a lampstand for the world to see the Light of Jesus.

I saw someone wearing a t-shirt that said, "Without Jesus I suck." God is the One who makes us amazing. Our testimony—our light—is His Presence manifest in us.

Sometimes we wonder, "Should church on Sunday be primarily for the saved or the unsaved?" In the Tabernacle we have an answer: it is for *both* fellowship with Christians *and* testimony to the world.

The purpose of testimony is to say, "Do it again, Lord!"

As Christians testify to God's goodness, we are praying for God to repeat that in others. Moreover, in addition to testifying individually, we also testify as a team. This is where the Church works together in ministry teams. The Holy Spirit empowers us with special abilities called spiritual gifts.

At first it may seem like we choose the ministry we would like to do. But during the course of our Christian journey, we eventually realize the Spirit chooses us.

There is a beautiful and life-giving Light that emanates from the Church. That Light is the Spirit of Jesus and the Church is His *Menora*, the Golden Lamp.

Summarize the Golden Lamp and its relationship between the Temple, Jesus, and you. _____

_____

The Golden Altar of Incense: Prayer

The focus of the Altar of Incense is prayer. But what is so remarkable about this station? It seems our whole journey has been one of prayer.

At the Bronze Altar we pray for salvation. At the Bronze Basin we pray for sanctification. At the Golden Table of Bread we pray the Living Word. At the Golden Lamp we pray that the light of our testimony might touch the world.

So why do we need a special station just for prayer?

For our fellowship with God to grow even more intimate, our prayer lives must go deeper.

As we grow in our prayer lives we do less talking and more listening.

41

We get better at asking the right questions. We press in to hear Him answer. We do not want to miss the still small voice of the Lord.

Each one us is designed to be an Altar of Incense. We were designed to hear His voice. We were made to intercede on behalf of the world. We stand before God to hear and obey His will. We stand on behalf of the people to make powerful petitions to God.

Summarize the Golden Altar of Incense and its relationship between the Temple, the Spirit, and you. _____

_____

The Altar of Incense is positioned just before the Ark of the Covenant. In prayer we petition God to do what only He can do—give us greater revelation of Himself. Only as we are attentive to His voice do we go from the Holy Place to the deepest place of intimacy with God—the Holy of Holies.

How do we encounter His Manifest Presence in the Holy Place? We encounter Him through one another. Through fellow Christians we experience His Presence.

It may be something a pastor or teacher says. It might be a conversation with someone at the meeting. It could happen in prayer or in worship. But we anticipate that moment when we know that we know that the Lord encountered us.

The result is we are built up. We grow stronger and more confident. We grow in Christ-like character. We are empowered with spiritual gifts. We are trained in the Word and Spirit. We are activated by the Spirit to reach out. In the Holy Place we are *equipped*.

Under the Old Covenant there was a large veil between the Holy Place and the Holy of Holies. However, at the Crucifixion of Christ, the veil was supernaturally torn in half from top to bottom. The blood of Jesus did what the blood of bulls and goats could never do. Jesus was the perfect Lamb of God who takes away the sin of the world.

Now through Jesus the Father beckons us into His Presence. The veil is removed because of the cross. Now nothing separates us from the love of God in Christ Jesus. The Father invites us into a personal audience with Him.

TRANSFORM

Remember, the Temple is our template for how to temple the Spirit.

From being *equipped* by His Presence in fellowship with the saints we now *transform* the world as we commune with God Himself. This was His plan all along.

In the Holy Place we experience His Presence in fellowship with other believers.

However, in the Holy of Holies you enter alone. No other person can commune with God on our behalf. Priests and pastors can only point you to Jesus. Fellow believers can testify to their own encounters with God. Here in the Holy of Holies you contend for *your* encounter with God.

Moses entered the Holy of Holies alone. The High Priest

entered the Holy of Holies alone once a year on Yom Kippur, the Day of Atonement.

Today, God invites you to a One on one encounter with His unveiled Presence 365 days a year, 7 days a week, 24 hours a day.

Today we can pray without ceasing. This is the place of deepest friendship with God. And we never have to leave His Presence. After all, we *temple the Spirit.*

Again, our Temple template helps us envision what it means to be a Temple. There appears to be only one item in the Holy of Holies, but we will discuss it in two parts: the Ark of the Covenant and the Mercy Seat. Since we are *Mishkan* Temples each of us come equipped with an Ark of the Covenant and Mercy Seat in our hearts.

The Ark of the Covenant: Spiritual Leadership

The Ark of the Covenant is a golden box that contains three items: the Ten Commandments, the Jar of Manna, and the Staff of Aaron. Each of these holds a vital key to living in the deepest place of communion with God.

Since this was the place where Moses, Aaron, and subsequent high priests met God, we are talking about Spiritual Leadership, or the leading of the Holy Spirit. Here we are not just talking about God's promptings for a leader's personal life. We are talking about downloads that God gives leaders in order to lead the people.

What does God have to say about how we become effective Spiritual leaders? How does God lead us so we can lead others? To answer these questions God placed three key items inside the Ark of the Covenant. Each item unlocks a key to being led by the Spirit of God. When *we* are being properly led by the Spirit, then we can effectively lead *others*.

> ## At the Ark of the Covenant God's message is clear: Spiritual Leadership requires a heart of obedience, faith, and authority.

A Heart Obedience

An excellent Spiritual leader is someone who has cultivated a heart of obedience to God. The Ten Commandments (or decalogue) characterize a heart of obedience that His Spirit now empowers us to live. The Ten Commandments were not given to unsaved people as a means of earning their salvation. Rather, they were given to a people already delivered by the supernatural grace of God so that they can cultivate a heart of obedience to follow the leadership of a holy God.

Ezekiel prophesied, "I will put My Spirit within you and cause you to walk in My statutes and you will be careful to observe My ordinances" (Ezekiel 36:27 NASB). Ezekiel prophesied a day when Israel would obey the Torah from the heart. That day has come! Now that His Spirit dwells within us we have a new heart to obey Him. We have the Ten Commandments in our hearts. If we will not obey the will of God, how can we live face to face with Him?

> ## If leaders will not obey God, how do they expect others to obey them?

The Spirit within us gives us a new desire to follow Jesus that wasn't there before. To be an excellent Spiritual

45

leader you first must be personally led by the Spirit. People need to follow leaders who get their marching orders from the Lord.

A Heart of Faith

An excellent Spiritual leader is someone who has cultivated a heart of faith in God. The Jar of Manna has to do with our dependency on God everyday.

Manna was food miraculously provided to the Israelites each morning while they were wandering in the wilderness. But it would only last a day. The following day the people had to have faith that the Lord would provide again.

The Lord taught us to pray, "Give us *this day* our *daily* bread." It does not mean the Bible is against long-term planning. Rather, we trust every plan to God.

German military planner Helmuth von Moltke said, "No battle plan survives contact with the enemy." To live in God's Presence means we have faith in Him to help us plan, but more importantly we have faith in Him for the outcome.

We do not get discouraged or lose heart if things don't go according to plan. We trust Him to provide for our daily needs.

If we have not cultivated a heart of faith in God, how will we follow Him into the bold and daring things He calls us to do? We are given a "Jar of Manna" every day that provides all the Spiritual sustenance we require.

Do we lack wisdom? Trust Him to give us wisdom. Do

we need finances? Trust Him to provide. Do we need
volunteers? Trust that He has already thought of that.

**Leaders do not worry about
what the future holds
but rather have faith in the One
who holds the future.**

A Heart of Authority

An excellent Spiritual leader is someone who has cultivated a heart of authority before God. The Staff of Aaron
underscores the importance of honoring the Spiritual
leaders God places in our lives. Before we can become a
Spiritual leader we must first honor the Spiritual leaders God places over us.

The people challenged the authority of Moses and
Aaron. So in Numbers 17 the Lord intervened to put a
stop to that. He caused Aaron's staff to supernaturally
bud, bloom, and bear almonds in the Tabernacle over
night. This astounded the rebellious leaders, and they
yielded to their God-appointed leaders, Moses and
Aaron.

To live face to face with God means we must honor the
Spiritual leaders He appoints. There are no perfect
Spiritual leaders. Christian parents are not perfect. And
as a pastor I can tell you that pastors are *far* from perfect. However, God appoints a "Staff of Aaron" to give us
authority to provide Spiritual direction.

**Leaders do not dishonor those
in Spiritual authority over them.**

This is so important to walking intimately with God that

He places the Staff of Aaron in the Ark of the Covenant. Does this mean we will always agree with our parents or pastors? No. But how many of us know there is an *honorable* way to disagree and a *dishonorable* way? By honoring our Spiritual leaders we honor God who appointed them. And this preserves our intimate fellowship with Jesus.

Each of us is designed with an Ark of the Covenant. We were made to embody the Ten Commandments, the Jar of Manna, and the Staff of Aaron in our lives. As we live face to face with almighty God we grow stronger and stronger in obedience, faith, and authority. Because we are being led by His Spirit, we can now help lead others to follow the leading of the Spirit.

Summarize the the Ark of the Covenant and its relationship between the Temple, the Spirit, and you. _____

_____

The Mercy Seat: Great Commission

The Mercy Seat is the seventh and final key to living face to face with God. This was the covering for the Ark of the Covenant. This was where Moses received His downloads from God.

It's not an actual seat for Moses to sit on. Instead, it represents the very Throne of God—the seat of power for all of existence.

Like Moses, Spiritual leaders are led by the Spirit in order to lead others in the Spirit.

It had two angels facing the center with their wings extended toward one another and their heads bowed.

So the Holy of Holies actually represents God's Throne Room and the Mercy Seat His Throne. We are now in the command center of the Universe.

What does the Mercy Seat have to do with transforming our world? Watch this. Once a year on Yom Kippur (The Day of Atonement), the High Priest would go beyond the veil and stand before the Mercy Seat.

Did you ever wonder what he was doing in there? Whatever he did in there had to be of the highest importance. After all he could only have this audience with God once a year!

Wearing the breastplate of the Twelve Tribes of Israel, the High Priest would sprinkle the sacred blood of a sacrificed goat on the Mercy Seat to atone for the sin of the nation of Israel. This foreshadows the blood of Jesus shed on behalf of the world.

In essence it is a Great Commission prayer for family, friends, your city, our country, and indeed the nations of the world. As the Royal Priesthood we are now commissioned to contend that all come under the rule of Christ the King.

Does it surprise us that the deepest place of intimacy with Jesus would fill us with compassion for the very people for whom He died? This is what we, the Royal Priesthood, do in the deepest recesses of God's heart.

Spiritual leaders contend for the nations to become disciples of Christ.

We are caught up in the passion of the Person and Purpose of Jesus in the Mercy Seat of our own heart. Are you seeking the Spirit of Jesus? You will find Him in the harvest!

Summarize the the Mercy Seat and its relationship between the Temple, Jesus, and you. _____

_____

The *Mishkan* Temple is where God and man meet. The Temple is our template for how to temple the Spirit. Today we are that Temple. In our Temple template we see that God takes us on an odyssey to connect, equip, and transform in order to take us to the place of deepest intimacy with Him and widest impact to the world. Through Jesus the secrets of the Temple have been unlocked. We can be living *Mishkan* Temples of His Presence on the Earth—*lightning in a bottle!*

By faith what did the Holy Spirit say to you in this section? How will you obey Him? _____

_____

Praxis

Body, Soul, & Spirit

Let's immediately try to make this practical for us. How do we as human beings function as the temple of the Holy Spirit?

Human beings were created body, soul, and spirit. I realize we use those words in many different ways today, so I will try to be more specific on what I mean by them.

With our physical bodies we relate to the *physical world*. At this very moment you might be sitting on a chair. You may be holding this book or reading it on some electronic device. You can interact with the physical world because you are a physical body. Pretty straightforward. When we hear people say, "Our body is a temple," they typically mean this. But human beings are much more than a physical body, aren't we.

What do I mean by soul? With our soul we relate to *ourselves*. David said, "Bless the Lord, O my soul" (Psalm 103:1 KJV). Who is he speaking to? He's talking to himself. He is saying to himself, "David, bless the Lord." If someone asks, "Mike, how are you today?"

I would do a quick inventory of my insides and most likely say, "Fine, thank you, how are you?" With our soul we relate to ourselves. (We can also relate to other souls on this level, but let's set that aside for now.) So our bodies are physical. Our souls are psychological. What about our spirit?

With our spirit we relate to God. Each one of us is a spirit. When the Bible says we were created in the image of God, it means we were patterned after His spiritual likeness. We were designed to relate to and interact with God! We are not bodies with a spirit; we are spirits with a body. One day our body will die, but our spirit will exist forever.

CS Lewis described us as *amphibians*—able to live in two environments. A frog hops on dry land but can also dive into a nearby pond and be perfectly at home in either environment. Perhaps we are more than amphibians. What creature can exist on land, water, and air? A duck! Or if you prefer, a swan, or some other water fowl. (How many of us know some Christians who are loons?) A swan can walk along the ground, paddle on the water, or at a moment's notice take to the air. Three realms.

In the same way, we can roam the physical world, explore our soul, and soar in the Spirit. We were wondrously designed to relate to the physical, psychological, and spiritual worlds. At first we may appear like ugly ducklings, but we can transform into beautiful swans.

What does it mean that human beings are body, soul, and spirit? _____

_____

The Human Temple
Before Salvation

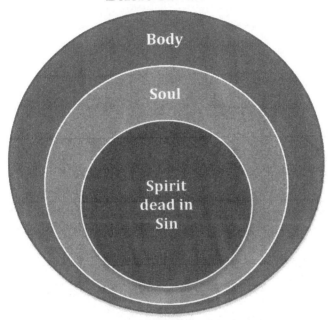

"Dead in your transgressions and sins" (Eph. 2:1 NIV)

Now catch this: Without Christ we are spiritually dead in our sins (Ephesians 2:1). We have no relationship with God. We live only for self.

When we come to Christ our spirit becomes instantly perfect, but our body and soul remain imperfect. If we had a broken arm before becoming a Christian, it will likely still be broken after we come to Christ. Can we be instantly healed? Sure. But if not, keep that cast on your arm. If we were fat before coming to Christ, we will still need to learn to eat healthy and exercise after coming to Christ. (And the Lord sure can teach us and empower us to lose weight!) Similarly, if we had emotional issues (e.g. rejection, anger, insecurity, fear, anxiety) before coming to Christ, we will probably have them after coming to Christ (unless instantly healed). We will all likely need to go through a *process* of Spiritual transformation to mitigate these issues both physical and emotional.

This is important to understand because many people assume that we become perfect after we accept Christ. So when we make a mistake we hear, "Hey! I thought you said you were a Christian?" And we feel ashamed. Or at work we feel like people are watching us more closely because we take a stand for Christ. And if we make a mistake they may say, "Coming in late...again? I thought you were a Christian. Hypocrite!" More shame. Or if we lose our temper at home our spouse will say, "Is that what they teach you in church?" Now we're embarrassed and really mad!

Can we see how this deflates a lot of believers who are told we are supposed to be the light of the world and the salt of the Earth? We quote St. Francis of Assisi: "Share Christ at all times and if necessary use words." But we suspect the message we are "sharing" carries little moral authority or integrity. The last thing we want to do now is "use words." "It may be better if no one here knows that I'm a Christian," we tell ourselves. Yet we keep reading in the Bible "make disciples of all nations" and "preach the gospel in season and out of season." And we feel stuck in the tension of being a less-than-perfect Christian witness.

However (and this is a HUGE "however"), there is one part of us that has been made completely and instantaneously perfect—our spirit. The believer is *spiritually* united with God by grace through the sacrifice of Jesus Christ on the cross.

In the instant that we invite the Lord Jesus into our hearts we are born again (John 3:16), we become a new creation (2 Corinthians 5:17), we become children of God (John 1:12), we are seated at the right hand of Christ (Ephesians 2:6), and we have the mind of Christ (1 Corinthians 2:16). All this occurs in the blink of an eye by the presence of the Holy Spirit within us. This is why one encounter with Jesus is so powerful. This is what we contend for on Sunday morning. By grace we become the *Mishkan* Temple of the Holy Spirit.

Our spirit is made instantly *perfect* by the righteousness of Jesus. In theological terms we say that the righteousness of Christ was *imputed* to us. Our spirit is not broken or fat. It does not suffer fear, anxiety, rejection, or insecurity. Our spirit has no anger management issues. Our spirit is now united with the Holy Spirit and it is perfect. In fact, it is the only part of us that is perfect. Our bodies and souls still have plenty of issues. Our spirit has none.

What is the one dimension of our being that is perfectly righteous? How is this possible? Why is this important?

_____

_____

The Human Temple
After Salvation

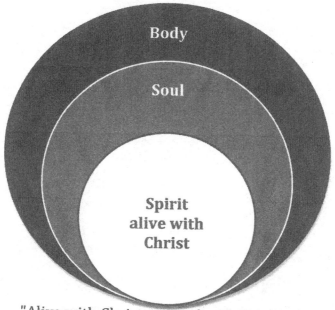

"Alive with Christ...seated with Him in the heavenly realms" (Ephesians 2:5-6)

We need to hear this, dear pilgrim! Do you know *where* your spirit is now that you have received Christ? Take a look at these passages from Paul that radically transformed the way I thought about myself.

"For he raised us from the dead along with Christ and seated us with him in the heavenly realms because we are united with Christ Jesus" (Ephesians 2:6 NLT).

Where is your spirit at this very moment? If you have received Jesus into your heart, then your spirit has been raised from the dead with Christ and *seated with Him in the heavenly realms.*

But if your spirit is now with Christ in the spiritual dimension, exactly where is the Spirit of Christ?

Watch this:

"I also pray that you will understand the incredible greatness of God's power...the same mighty power that raised Christ from the dead and seated him in the place of honor *at God's right hand* (italics mine) in the heavenly realms" (Ephesians 1:19-20 NLT).

OMG! Did you catch that?

Jesus is seated in the place of honor at God's right hand in the spiritual dimension. This means that your spirit —YOU— are *right there* in the heavenly court! Jesus sits in the seat of honor at the right hand of the Father and you, my friend, are in a seat by Him.

This is why Paul exhorts us to live from the Spirit not the flesh. Our bodies and souls still have issues, but our spirits are perfect in Christ Jesus.

After salvation where is the "location" of our spirit? Why is this important to transforming our soul and body? _____

_____

Who can set us free from the power of sin in our body and soul? Of course the answer is Jesus but allow me to illustrate how He does this.

As one who temples the Spirit, we now have the ability to receive personal downloads from God. Imagine the spiritual dimension is God's wifi. How many of us know there are "messages" being broadcast all around us all the time? But we can't see or hear them. There are countless radio stations playing music right now but you can't hear them. Why? Because you're not a radio. There are multiple television stations broadcasting now but you can't watch them. Why? Because you're not a TV.

You are, however, a *Mishkan* Temple of the Holy Spirit!

As the *Mishkan* Temple of the Spirit you now have the capacity to access God's wifi.

Jesus Himself said, "My sheep hear My voice" (John 10:27 NASB). We were born for the purpose of knowing, loving, and relating to God. We were made in His spiritual image. We may not even know exactly how we do it, but we do. He grants us access into His spiritual wifi. But we'll need the password. The password is "Jesus."

What is God's wifi? How do we gain access? Why is this important? _____

_____

Although our body and soul still have issues, our spirit has been made perfectly new in Christ Jesus. There is one dimension of us that is in a perfect relationship with God—our spirit. This is what "new creation in Christ" means.

The Human Temple
After Salvation Under Attack

"Flaming arrows of the evil one" (Ephesians 6:16)
attack only body and soul not our spirit.

Now here's an important question: When we come under attack from the enemy or the world, which dimensions of us come under attack? Scripture is clear that nothing can separate us from the love of God in Christ Jesus. Our spirit man is invincible inasmuch as the Holy Spirit is invincible. That means our spirit is really really invincible! Our spirit is imputed with the righteous perfection of Jesus.

However, our body and soul still have issues. This is where we get attacked. The enemy cannot attack our spirit where the Holy Spirit resides, but he can go after our body and soul.

The enemy aims his fiery arrows at our thoughts and feelings, where? In our soul. Satan and the world can also attack our body through sickness, pain, and suffering.

For example, the enemy might say, "God doesn't love you. Your spouse doesn't love. You are a failure." It's really easy to discern the voice of the devil because he fills our soul with feelings of rejection, insecurity, anxiety, hatred, lust, greed, envy, etc. And Job can tell us all about how the devil goes after our body.

What dimensions of us does the enemy attack? How do we overcome his attacks? _____

_____

But remember that our spirit is connected with Jesus. Our spirit is the only part of us that is brand new and perfect. So now from the Holy Spirit who speaks to our spirit, we know the truth. The Spirit dispels the devil's lies. The devil's deceptions are broken by the revelation we receive from the Holy Spirit.

The Spirit says, "God *does* love you and will never leave you or forsake you. Your spouse loves you too (for now, anyway, so get your act together). And you are not a failure (but you might be if you don't listen to Me right now)."

It's not hard to discern the voice of the Spirit because He fills our soul with love, joy, peace, patience, kindness, gentleness, goodness, faithfulness, and self-control. We find new hope in the Spirit along with conviction, courage, strength, and honor. He restores our soul and brings healing to our body.

He not only tells us the truth, He empowers us to make the right choices to live in freedom and keep our lives in alignment with God's will. His love fills us with zeal and passion for the things of the Spirit. Before Jesus we were not interested in the Bible, Church, worship, or evangelism. But now He gives us new desires we never had before. We hunger for His Word. We look forward to Church. We long for His Presence in worship. We are full of compassion for people who don't know Jesus. His overflowing love fills us with the power to choose the things of the Spirit.

The power of Spirit-empowered choices transforms our body and soul.

That said, here's something that needs to be addressed. Some say that discipleship (obedient living) is the key to freedom. Others say that deliverance (overcoming demonization) is the key. Who is right?

During the course of our spiritual journey we may come across those who seem to believe the devil is behind everything that goes wrong. On the opposite side of the spectrum, there are those who completely ignore the devil's hand in anything.

In reality, however, we will never be able to "deliver" a person who simply will not take a stand and obey the Lord. In the same vein, we will never be able to "disciple" a person who is demonized.

We need to diagnose the problem prayerfully and apply the right remedy. This is why we need Spiritual discernment as we minister. If a person is never able to get set free from an issue he's been fighting for years, why not explore the possibility of demonization. A spiritual stronghold is something that has a *strong hold* on us. Jesus cast out plenty of demons while He was on the Earth. Did the world suddenly become devoid of demons? I don't think so.

Then there are those who keep getting "delivered" but never get set free. The reason? They simply will not "work out" their salvation. They refuse to go to God's Word daily to have their minds renewed. They refuse to make fundamental choices to live in freedom.

We will never be able to "deliver" someone who refuses to obey the Lord, and we will never be able to "disciple" someone who is demonized.

How do we diagnose the situation properly? How do we know which remedy to apply? All the discernment we need to live free flows from the living streams of the Holy Spirit who now resides in our spirit. Let's not forget that both discipleship and deliverance are powered by the Holy Spirit, not by human effort. Both are made possible because we are the *Mishkan* Temple.

Imagine the living waters of the Spirit extinguishing the fiery arrows of the enemy. The Spirit brings healing over emotional wounds. He shows us whom we need to forgive. He shows us from whom we need forgiveness. He empowers us to walk with a spirit of repentance.

The Human Temple
Living in Freedom

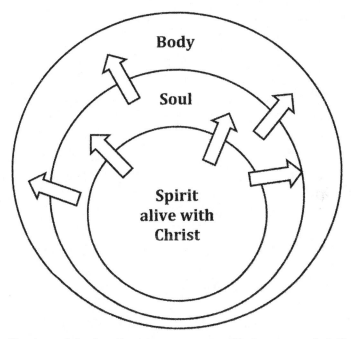

Extinguish the flaming arrows (Ephesians 6:16)

The Holy Spirit can reveal to us if some part of our soul has a demonic stronghold.   Through Spirit-directed prayer, these strongholds are broken.

How does the Spirit extinguish the fiery attacks of the enemy? _____

_____

At our Church we like to say we have the best prayer ministry in the known galaxy.   Supernatural insights, words and pictures come to different members of the team. Often the Spirit will show them something that happened a long time ago in a person's past—an entry point for the demonic. Then through repentance and forgiveness, people are set free. The Spirit brings deliverance through the Church.

Moreover, the Spirit empowers us to *work out* our salvation in fear and trembling. Through discipleship relationships we hold one another accountable to live in freedom. A good Spiritual mentor will know how to ask the right questions to lead a disciple to self-discovery. This must occur by mutual consent. Cults use authoritarian methods of discipleship. A healthy discipleship relationship is one that remembers that both mentor and disciple are disciples of Christ.

The living waters of the Spirit spring forth and wash over our soul and body, breaking lies and deception and renewing our minds with biblical truth.

How do deliverance and discipleship help us live in freedom? _____

_____

When is the phrase "filled with the Spirit" first used in Scripture? Here's the passage:

"Now the Lord spoke to Moses, saying, 'See, I have called by name Bezalel, the son of Uri, the son of Hur, of the tribe of Judah. I have filled him with the Spirit of God in wisdom, in understanding, in knowledge, and in all *kinds of* craftsmanship'" (Exodus 31:1-3 NASB).

The first time we see the phrase "filled with the Spirit" is in the context of building the *Mishkan*. God gives

Moses specific direction on how He wants him to build the *Mishkan*. Then God appoints the artists to build them. These men, Bezalel, the Chief Craftsman, and Oholiab, his assistant, are especially *gifted* by the Holy Spirit to create the items with excellence and precision.

The Holy Spirit must be the One who empowers us to build our *Mishkan* Temple. Only a person filled with the Holy Spirit can be transformed into a Temple of the Spirit. Being transformed into a Temple of the Spirit will require some engineering and craftsmanship. It is more art than science, a creative process rather than assembly line mass production. We will need to be led and built by His Spirit. The Holy Spirit Himself superintends the creation of His own dwelling place on the Earth.

Where is the Bible's first reference to being "filled with the Spirit?" Why is this important? _____

_____

This means we will need to grow in our capacity to discern the voice of the Holy Spirit amidst all the other voices in our heads. We cooperate with the Spirit of God as He transforms us into His Temple. There are many voices in our heads. It doesn't mean we're crazy. This is perfectly normal. Allow me to illustrate.

It's Sunday morning. You need to wake up early to go to Church. But your body says to you, "Just five more minutes please! We're so tired!" The body speaks in terms of urges and appetites, in this case, sleep.

Your soul chimes in, "Yeah, we don't *feel* like getting up now." This is the language of the soul—it's all about what you *feel* like doing or don't *feel* like doing.

But remember there is one dimension of us that is in a perfect relationship with God—our spirit. And the Holy Spirit informs our spirit and says, "Wake up and go to Church! Besides, you're the pastor, so go to Church!"

Describe how to navigate the different voices in our head. _____

_____

Some might call this our conscience. Let's explore that biblically for a moment to gain more clarity on the conscience.

The Greek word for conscience is *syneidesis*, which comes from the root word *synoida*, which means "I know together with." Our conscience is not God, but it is that part of our heart that can listen to God. Isn't it amazing that our minds were created with the capacity to "know something in common with God?"

In fact, Hebrew does not have a unique word for "conscience" and instead refers to it as "heart" (1 Samuel 24:5), leaving the translator to determine its meaning through context.

It is super important to know that since conscience is not God but rather a part of us, it can be weakened and defiled (1 Corinthians 8:7), wounded (1 Corinthians 8:12), seared and rendered virtually useless (1 Timothy 4:2). Thank God for the Holy Spirit who dwells within the believer to give him a "perfectly good conscience" (Acts 23:1 Cf. 1 Peter 3:16).

Jesus said, "My sheep hear My voice." Then He continues, "And I know them, and they follow Me" (John 10:27 NASB). Do you see how we need to sift through the many voices in our head to get to the voice of Jesus in order to follow Him?

Let's not forget that there are also the voices of other people in our head. Sometimes God speaks through them. Many times He doesn't. There are also demonic voices. But remember, "Greater is He who is in you than he who is in the world" (1 John 4:4 NASB). In other words, God's ability to lead you is greater than the devil's ability to mislead you.

The key is to know the "still small voice of God." How do we do that? The key is to live from the "Mind of Christ." The Mind of Christ can never be weakened, defiled, wounded, seared, or rendered useless. Our human conscience can, but the Mind of Christ remains perfect. It is, after all, the Mind of CHRIST.

Everyone is born with a conscience, but you must be born again to have the Mind of Christ.

What is the difference between the Mind of Christ and our conscience? Why is it important to maintain a clear conscience? _____

The Mind of Christ

"We have the Mind of Christ" (1 Corinthians 2:16 NASB).

The context of 1 Corinthians 2 is important. It leads us to an amazing reality. Paul is essentially stating a well-known fact: no one can read a person's mind. We don't know what other people are thinking. Only the *spirit* of the person knows what he's thinking.

In the same way, who can know the thoughts of God? Only the Spirit of God can know the Mind of God. So what happens if we've been given the Spirit of God? That's right! We can know the thoughts of God! We have the Mind of Christ.

Paul is giving us a powerful revelation. The Lord has extended an amazing privilege to us! He invites us to think with His thoughts. He wants us to have His heart on every matter.

Now, I don't know anyone who knows the Mind of God perfectly. We get a flicker here, a glimmer there. Sometimes it's like trying to recall the face of an old classmate from first grade. "We see through a glass darkly." Nevertheless, there it is—through the Holy Spirit we can know the thoughts of God. We have the Mind of Christ.

To be clear Paul is not advocating a "psychic" approach to knowing God's will apart from the written word of God. We must be *"Anchored to God's word and led by His Spirit."* (The motto of my Church, New Hope Central Oahu). The Apostles said, "But we will devote ourselves to prayer and to the ministry of the word" (Acts 6:4 NASB). Through the word and prayer the Mind of Christ transforms us.

I should also note that this is not some kind of self-improvement plan. The Mind of Christ is not something *we* develop. We do not "train" ourselves to have it. We do not apply certain principles or methods to attain it. It is not an objective to accomplish. It's not like we can say, "My goal is to form the Mind of Christ." These things may apply to our conscience but not the Mind of Christ.

Rather, the Mind of Christ is the by-product of being in relationship with Jesus. The Mind of Christ is ours by the grace of God. It is God's doing, not something we earned. We already have it by reason of His Presence within us. We have the Mind of Christ because we Temple the Spirit. And we Temple the Spirit because of how much He loves us and desires to be with us. Therefore, it is a matter of cooperating with our heavenly Father.

Do you want to know what the voice of God sounds like? He sounds like the Bible! Indeed, it is through the study of Scripture that we grow more intimate with how Jesus thinks and how His voice sounds. The Bible gives us excellent history of how God spoke to our forebears. The Bible also provides us with time-honored, non-negotiable principles to live by.

I recall the first time I went through the entire Bible back in college. I was determined not to just read through it but *study* the whole Bible. I used Alan Stibbs' *Search the Scriptures*, a personal three-year Bible study (that took me four years to finish!). Subsequent to that I've been using various "Bible-in-a-year" devotional guides, the New Hope SOAP Journaling method, not to mention years of formal (expensive!) training.

One of the conclusions of my search through the Scriptures is this: God still speaks today. He never stopped speaking. As we read about different biblical characters, how do we know which biblical example applies to our current predicament? The Father will tell us. As we learn biblical principles, how do we know which applies

to our situation? The Spirit will reveal this to us. How?
Through the Mind of Christ.

Like Paul, we are contending for a "demonstration of the
Spirit and of power" (1 Corinthians 2:4 NASB).

One second in the Manifest Presence of God can transform us more than 30 years of sitting in church.

When we have an encounter with the Spirit of Jesus, we
will never be the same again. The purpose of having the
Mind of Christ is so we can discern what God is up to
and participate. Look for the encounter.

Describe the last encounter you had with God. How
did it transform your life? _____

_____

So how do we *Temple the Spirit* vis-à-vis the Mind of
Christ? I approach it as a Spiritual discipline. We never
practice a Spiritual discipline to merit or earn God's
favor. Rather, a Spiritual discipline clears a pathway for
God to move and speak.

Here's what you do. In prayer ask the Lord to command
all other voices to be silent. Ask the Lord to empower
you to silence the voice of your physical body—your
appetite for food, sleep, sex, etc.

Then ask Him to silence the voice of your soul—so it
doesn't become about what you *feel* like doing or don't
feel like doing.

Next ask the Spirit to silence the voices of people. This

is where you might do something (or don't do some-thing) out of a fear of man, i.e., a fear of what people think.

Shut off the voices of radio, television, gaming, social media, etc.

Then ask the Lord to silence the voice of the demonic.

As all these voices go silent, you become more sensi-tized to the still small voice of the Lord.

Finally pray this: "Speak, Father, your child is listening."

Remember Star Trek: The Original Series, Season 1: Episode 20: "Court Martial" which aired February 2, 1967. (Thank you, Wikipedia!) Capt. Kirk was on trial for accidentally killing Lt. Commander Ben Finney. Turns out that Finney was alive. He had an old grudge against Kirk and was trying to frame him. Remember how Dr. McCoy proved that Finney was still alive? Bones used an auditory sensor that tracked the sound of every heartbeat on the ship. Then he systematically eliminat-ed the heartbeat of every *known* person. When he was done they could still hear the heartbeat of one person unaccounted for—Finney. The Spiritual discipline of the Mind of Christ reminds me of that episode. We system-atically eliminate all other voices in order to hear the still small voice of the Spirit.

The Mind of Christ Spiritual discipline would be excel-lent to practice before studying the Bible, before going to Church, before staff meetings, before going to a party, before going to the movies, before you get into a fight with your spouse, before you yell at the other motorists on the road, before you get out of bed, and before you go to sleep. In other words 24 hours a day!

By practicing this discipline before Bible study, we avoid a merely academic exercise and tune into the Lord speaking to us through the Scriptures.

By practicing this discipline before interacting with people, we minimize fleshly words and contend for speaking with words and a tone laced with the fruit of the Spirit.

By practicing this discipline before watching a movie, we guard our hearts from temptation and might even see a Jesus-like character somewhere on the screen. How many of us know that there's a Jesus-like character in just about every movie?

By practicing this discipline before staff meetings, we diminish human agendas and augment the will of God.

By practicing this discipline before getting out of bed, we capitalize on that brief moment when our thoughts are lucid yet neutral and we have not yet taken back control of our prayers.

By practicing this discipline before going to sleep, we tune into dreams—one of God's favorite ways to speak to us.

What is the Spiritual discipline of the Mind of Christ? How does it work? _____

_____

"For the mind set on the flesh is death, but the mind set on the Spirit is life and peace, because the mind set on the flesh is hostile toward God; for it does not subject itself to the law of God, for it is not even able *to do so*, and those who are in the flesh cannot please God" (Romans 8:6-8 NASB).

By practicing the Mind of Christ discipline, we are poised to set our mind on the Spirit who dwells within us. We become a functioning *Mishkan* Temple of the Spirit. The voices of the flesh are hostile toward God and lead to death—the death of churches, the death of families, the death of marriages. But proceeding from the Mind of Christ is life giving. This leads to healthy churches, loving families, and happy marriages.

What is the side of your forehead called? It is appropriately called the "temple." So when someone comes up with a great idea, he might point to his temple with a grin on his face. When you think of it, that's a great name for our minds. When we live from the Mind of Christ, we *Temple the Spirit.*

If you're like me you need books to get to the point pretty quickly, so I tried to do that in this first section. But I also find that once I fully engage the Lord in an important subject—like becoming *lighting in a bottle*—my curiosity level goes up. I want to know more details. So if you continue reading, this next section is for people like us.

By faith what did the Holy Spirit say to you in this section? How will you obey Him? _____

_____

Prayer
In the Temple Courts

"If you talk to a man in a language he understands, that goes to his head. If you talk to him in his own language, that goes to his heart." Nelson Mandela

The Temple is God's own "language." As we speak God's language, our desire is to touch His heart. In the same vein when God spoke to Moses, He spoke Hebrew. Obviously, God "speaks" every human tongue, but I think there is something very special and intimate about praying to God in His original tongue. God chose the Hebrew language, culture, and people to speak to us. I have included some of my favorite prayers in Hebrew on our prayer walk through the Temple courts.

The Outer Court

O Lord, I eagerly seek Your face this day, passionately, with all my heart, soul, mind, and body. I have set the course of my whole being to know you intimately. As the sun rises at my back, I see the Temple before me glowing with the dawn.

Modeh 'ani lefaneykha,
I come before you with thanksgiving

Melekh chai veqaiyam
King living and eternal

Shehechezarta bi nishmati bechemlah
For you returned my soul to me in compassion

Rabbah emunatekha
Great is Your faithfulness![1]

Lord Jesus, my body and soul are Your *Mishkan* Temple. My heart is Your home. This is our house where you and I dwell together as Father and child. Even as I have welcomed Your Presence in My life, so too I see You, Jesus, inviting me in, and I walk into the Outer Court. I worship and adore You, Lord. I bow down before You. This is where You and I first CONNECT.

Station 1: The Bronze Altar
Lord, I stand before the Bronze Altar.

You take me back to the day I first met You, the day of my salvation. I behold You on the cross. I am filled with the fear of God as I see the terrible consequence of my sin. But I am also overwhelmed with awe at Your grace. While I was yet Your enemy, You died for me.

Adonai kitov, ki leolam hasdo.
The Lord is good, His loving-kindness endures forever.

Your grace is truly amazing! You have placed Your precious blood on the doorpost of my heart. The Angel of Death has passed over me. O glorious day! O glorious day! The day of my freedom! My carnal self was crucified with You. Now I am resurrected with You a brand new person! Because of You, Jesus, I stand righteous and blameless before You, though I know I deserved the exact opposite. I connect with You only because You first came to seek and save me, even when my heart was far from You. I am perfectly loved before I have become perfectly lovable. I am accepted before I am acceptable. Lord Jesus, your salvation is the greatest gift I have ever received.

Station 2: The Bronze Basin
Next I behold the Bronze Basin.

Lord, because of the power of Your love, my spirit is now one with Your Spirit. But I see a different law still at war in my soul and body. I do not always think what I ought to think. I do not always speak what I should speak. I do not always do what I want to do.

Wash me, Holy Spirit, in the living streams of Sanctification. I resolve not to be conformed to this world, but to be transformed by the renewing of my mind. I want us to connect on every level, so heal my issues, Lord. Cross examine my heart so I love what You love and hate what You hate. Heal my emotions, Lord, from the hurts of the past, that I might love again with holy abandon.

My heart overflows with gratitude as Your Spirit sets me free! I may not be perfect but Your Spirit teaches me to forgive myself, to forgive others, and to walk in the freedom of reconciliation.

The Holy Place
Lord, I enter the Temple and stand in the Holy Place.

Now I am better prepared to interact with my brothers and sisters in the Holy Place. In the Holy Place I seek Your Presence with my Spiritual family.

Everything is golden in the Holy Place.

Because You have forgiven me, I can forgive others. Because I have been set free from myself, I am free from others. I will not be provoked by anything they do or say. Because of Your love, joy, and peace, I am un-provokable and un-offendable. EQUIP us now, Lord, to love one another as You have loved us that the world will know that we are Your disciples.

Station 3: The Golden Table of Bread
Lord, we walk to the right side of the Holy Place to the Golden Table of Bread.

Lord, we welcome You as the Bread of Life. Your Manifest Presence is food to our souls! For we do not live only by putting bread in our mouths, but by the Spiritual Bread that comes forth from the mouth of God.

Thank you for Your Word, O God. The Bible is indeed Holy to us! For as we read, hear, study, and memorize Your written Word, we are better equipped to walk with You, our Living Word. We hear Your voice in the Scriptures and move in consonance with Your will.

Station 4: The Golden Lamp
Lord, together we walk to the Golden Lamp.

You have brought us out of darkness into Your marvelous Light. Now our lives shimmer with Your Shekhinah glory. We will be Your Menorah revealing Your Way,

Truth, and Life to a dark world. May our good works shine for You now, Jesus.

Equip us to testify to the world, to minister together as a team.

Station 5: The Golden Altar of Incense
Lord, now we gather around the Golden Altar Incense. Here we offer up a sacrifice of praise and worship to the Name who is above all names!

Baruch Hashem
Blessed be the Name!

Your Spirit prays through our earthen vessels with an utterance beyond mortal words. Our prayers ascend to the angel with the bowl who will mingle them with the incense of Heaven. Fire! Fire from Your holy altar ignites the incense and our prayers! The angel pours the bowl out upon the Earth. The power of God is unleashed —salvations, signs, wonders, miracles, and healing! Lightning fills our bottles with the Presence and Power of the Almighty!

The Holy of Holies
Jesus, You have torn the veil that separated me from Your Presence. Lord, I come into Your golden Presence in the Holy of Holies. I have come at Your behest to have a face-to-face encounter with You. Leaving my brothers and sisters in the Holy Place, You and I are now One on one.

Lord, I am in awe of You, of the access You have granted me. But for the grace of God, I am here and I am not destroyed. My spirit is transformed by Your Spirit.

Make me an instrument to TRANSFORM others.

Station 6: The Ark of the Covenant

Lord, I behold the Ark of the Covenant. Your Presence is golden! I embrace Your Spirit that empowers and leads me, that I might be a Spirit-led, servant leader to others. Thank You for Your Ten Commandments and a heart of obedience. I incline My ear now to hear Your voice.

Aseret Hadiberot

The Ten Commandments

'Anokhi Adonai 'Eloheikha
I AM the Lord your God.

Lo' ihiyeh lekha 'elohim 'acherim `al panai
You shall have no other gods before My face.

Lo' tissa 'et shem Adonai 'eloheikha lash shav
You shall not carry the Name of the Lord Your God in vain.

Zakhor 'et yom hash shabat leqadesho
Remember the Sabbath Day to keep it holy.

Kabbed 'et 'avikha ve 'et imekha
Honor your father and your mother.

Lo' tir-tsach
You shall not murder.

Lo' tin'af
You shall not commit adultery.

Lo' tignov
You shall not steal.

Lo' ta`aneh bere`akha `ed shaqer
You shall not bear false witness against anyone.

Lo' tachmod
You shall not covet.[2]

Thank You for the Jar of Manna and a heart of faith.
Thank You for the Staff of Aaron and a heart of authority.

By these I am a transforming life who transforms lives.
Spirit fill me, speak to me, lead me. Abba, I am Your
child and Your servant who hears Your voice and obeys
Your will with faith and authority.

Station 7: The Mercy Seat
Covering the Ark of the Covenant I behold the Mercy
Seat.

The Throne of Heaven! And He who sits on the throne!
With the angelic hosts of Heaven I declare:

"Holy! Holy! Holy! Heaven and Earth are filled with Your
glory!" May the nations worship the Name above all
names! Every knee shall bow and every tongue confess
that You are Lord of lords and King of kings!

Baruch atta Adonai Eloheinu Melekh haolam
Blessed are you Lord our God King of the universe!

In Jesus' glorious Name I make disciples of the nations!
By the One who has all authority in Heaven and Earth, I
make disciples who make disciples who make disciples
so the nations will bring glory, honor, and blessing with
all their heart, soul, mind, and strength to the One who

alone is worthy to receive all praise and adoration.

Hallelujah! Hallelujah! Hallelujah! Hallelujah!

'El Melekh ne 'eman
God our faithful King!

Amen and amen.

---

1. Parsons, John. *Zola's Introduction to Hebrew,* Zola Levitt Ministries, Inc. (Dallas, TX), 2011, p. 244. Also, www.Hebrew4Christians.com
2. ibid., pp. 225-229.

Part 1

The Outer Court

CONNECT

The Outer Court

CONNECT

It is a glorious morning as the sun rises in the east. You are standing outside the gate of the Temple with the dawn at your back. The Temple shimmers in the sunlight as you approach the Outer Court. This is where your journey begins—the most critical odyssey you will ever undertake in your whole life.

Indeed, it is the purpose of your existence. You were born to go on this journey—to search for God. From the moment you came into this world you knew of His existence. As you gazed into the night sky, the Universe spoke to you of its Creator. You knew *about* Him but you did not know Him.

Eternity pulsates with every beat of your heart.

But how can the finite know the Infinite? How can a mortal know the Eternal? How can an Earth-bound breach the barriers of Heaven?

You have one hope: That God would allow Himself to be found. "But who am I that God would take any interest in me?" Does God want to know me?" Yes! He made the Temple for the expressed purpose of having a place where you and He could meet—*connect.* He knows your limitations better than you. He created this place to take you beyond your human limitations.

Here your mortality will be fused with His Divinity. The result will not make you a demigod but rather fully human. This is your destiny: to become fully yourself. And as you become yourself you reflect the image of God imprinted on you from conception.

As you step into the Outer Court you are immediately confronted with a Bronze Altar. Its fire comes from a supernatural source. Behind it, a Bronze Basin filled with pure water. Everything so far is bronze.

Bronze is beautiful, but it is not to be mistaken for gold. You are in search of the gold, but to get there you must first deal with the bronze.

There is an Outer Court within each of us—a place where we first encounter Jesus. As you enter this sacred place, listen to the Spirit whisper in your heart, "Welcome."

Why do you think God designed you with an Outer Court? _____

_____

Chapter 1
The Bronze Altar: Salvation

"Salvation is found in no one else, for there is no other name under Heaven given to mankind by which we must be saved" (Acts 4:12 NIV).

Remember our thesis: By understanding God's design of the *Mishkan* Temple as His way of taking us on an odyssey to *connect*, *equip*, and *transform*, we can grow in our intimacy with the Person and mission of Jesus and embrace how we too can *temple* the Holy Spirit.

The word "altar" means "lifted up." It comes from the Latin word "alta" which indicates a high place, as in "altitude." The Hebrew word for altar is "mizbeah" which means "place of sacrifice." So the patriarchs of the Bible would typically go up to a high place to make their sacrifices to God. Therefore, whenever you see the word "altar" that implies a sacrifice must be made.

What does the word "altar" imply? _____

_____

Jesus said, "And when I am lifted up from the Earth, I

will draw everyone to Myself" (John 12:32 NLT). Jesus is the ultimate sacrifice for the sin of mankind. Salvation is found in no one else. But salvation is a huge word. It goes way beyond a free pass to Heaven.

In a sense the whole design of the Temple is about the salvation Jesus provides. He is the first and the last, the alpha and the omega. So Jesus is the central figure at the beginning of our journey here at the Bronze Altar, and He is our final destination at the Mercy Seat. Every station provides a dimension of salvation. According to God's design, we are introduced to Jesus at the Bronze Altar. What does that mean exactly? Let's find out.

At its core did you know that the Jewish faith is really a message of grace? Abraham was saved by grace not works. "Abraham believed the Lord and He credited it to him as righteousness" (Genesis 15:6; cf. Romans 4:3; Galatians 3:6; James 2:23). To be sure the Jews had their problems with legalists much like Christians do. There is always someone who will argue that salvation is by faith plus work. This is what Mormons, Jehovah's Witnesses, and every cult will teach. Indeed every world religion not based on the Bible teaches this. Only the Judeo-Christian faith is unique in this matter, and for good reason.

So imagine yourself walking into the Outer Court from the east. We're on the greatest adventure of our lives—an odyssey to the deepest place of intimacy with God. Like Indiana Jones we discover an ancient map that shows us the layout of the Temple, inscribed by a prophet who had one-on-one conversations with God. If anyone would know the way, he would.

On our map the first thing that confronts us is a Bronze

Altar. According to Exodus 27 this was a 7½-foot square box 4½ feet high. It was made of acacia wood but overlaid with bronze. Sometimes we might see it described as a "brazen" or "brass" altar. Brazen, brass, and bronze all mean basically the same thing here. The Bronze Altar had four horns, one on each corner. Horns always symbolize the power of God. Paul said, "I am not ashamed of the Gospel, for it is the power of God for salvation" (Romans 1:16 NASB). Jesus is the horn of God's salvation.

Through the Bronze Altar the Lord revealed to His people that the penalty for sin is death, but the blood of an innocent could be shed on behalf of the guilty.

And there it is—salvation by the grace of God in the Jewish faith! The people would bring an unblemished animal from their herds. It could be cattle, sheep, or a goat. They would then place their hand on its head. Why? "Lay your hand on the animal's head, and the Lord will accept its death in your place to purify you" (Leviticus 1:4 NLT). The animal would pay with its life for the person's sin. It would be slaughtered before God and the priests for all to see. Its blood would be splattered on the sides of the altar, then its body burned as a sacrifice. Year after year this bloody scene would repeat. Time after time the people would reflect on the horrific price for disobeying God...and what it took to be reconciled with Him.

What is the significance of the Bronze Altar and how is it related to Jesus? _____

_____

"The life of a creature is in the blood" (Leviticus 17:11 NIV). Let's briefly discuss the connection between life and blood. There is something deeply spiritual and powerful about blood. The first murder in history occurred when Cain murdered his brother, Abel. Afterward God confronted Cain, "What have you done? The voice of your brother's blood is crying out to me from the ground!" (Genesis 4:10 NET). Blood has a spiritual voice. Abel's life-blood cried out to God from the ground. The voice of Abel's blood said, "Injustice!"

What is the Spiritual significance of blood in the Bible?

_____

_____

Fast forward to Jesus who said, "Whoever eats my flesh and drinks my blood has eternal life" (John 6:54 NIV). Jesus says that by His blood we will have eternal life. All of us are born in sin because of Adam. Adam's blood within every man cries out, "Unrighteous!" Jesus' blood, on the other hand, cries out, "Stamped with My righteousness!" In the Spirit once we receive a transfusion of the blood of Jesus, the righteous blood of Jesus replaces the unrighteous blood of Adam. And since the "life is in the blood," we now have eternal life through Christ Jesus.

There is a precious lady in our Church named Cindy. She has a sister named Sandy who was dying of leukemia—cancer of the blood. Her blood was killing her. She needed to be able to produce healthy blood cells. This meant that she needed a bone marrow transplant. It turns out that Cindy was a perfect match for her sister. After grueling and painful hours of harvesting bone marrow from Cindy's body, doctors then transplanted the healthy bone marrow into Sandy. The procedure was a success! Both Cindy and Sandy recovered wonderfully. And now Sandy is cured of cancer.

The procedure, however, left them both with an amazing side effect: Now Sandy's DNA is almost 100% identical to Cindy's DNA! Life is in the blood. Sandy now has Cindy's life-blood flowing through her. Cindy's blood continues to save Sandy's life to this day. Sandy survives today because her old DNA is gone and now she has Cindy's DNA. She had to literally become a different person in order to live.

Listen, this is what the blood of Jesus does for all who believe. When God looks upon us now, our blood no longer cries out "unrighteous." Instead, the Father sees us with a whole new life and a new identity. When He looks upon us, He no longer sees us in our sinful state. He doesn't see Adam, He sees Jesus! It is the Spirit of Jesus who dwells within us now.

We now have the spiritual DNA of Jesus, and this opens the door to a universe of new possibilities.

When a person comes to Jesus whose spiritual DNA do they have now? Why is this important? _____

_____

There is a Bronze Altar in every human heart. From the moment we came into existence we looked up at the universe and knew there was Someone out there greater than ourselves. We also became painfully aware that the world was broken, that we were broken. We instinctively knew that in terms of morality we were fallen.

Humanity must come to terms with the Bronze Altar in its heart. So Buddhism offers its Eightfold Path to Enlightenment; Islam, its Five Pillars. Atheists desperately argue the Bronze Altar doesn't exist, but their conscience tells them otherwise.

What will satisfy? What will assuage the deep existential conviction within every human heart?

Only the Designer of the Bronze Altar can fulfill the purpose for which it was designed. Even the Jewish sacrificial system was merely a foreshadowing of what was to come. "For it is impossible for the blood of bulls and goats to take away sins" (Hebrews 10:4 ESV). So God Himself must provide the Ram. And this is why God sent the Son, the only begotten of the Father. He would offer Himself as the perfect sacrifice for the sin of mankind. God provided the Ram. His name is Jesus, the Lamb of God. "Behold! The Lamb of God who takes away the sin of the world!" (John 1:29 NKJV).

What is the significance of every human heart being designed with a Bronze Altar? _____

_____

There is something very important you should know about the Bronze Altar. The salvation we receive here comes exclusively by the Hand of God. Jesus freely offered His life. Pilate, the Romans, the Jewish leaders, Judas, and the angry mob had no power over Him beyond what was prophesied and permitted. With His last breath, the Lord said to Abba, "Into Thy hands I commit My Spirit. It is finished." He voluntarily sacrificed His life for us.

Now watch this. So in the same way it was the Lord Himself who lit the fire of the Bronze Altar. "The glory of the Lord appeared to the whole community. Fire blazed forth from the Lord's presence and consumed the burnt offering...on the altar" (Lev. 9:23-24 NLT). The people built the *Mishkan* exactly as God command-ed. They made every piece of furnishing according to specifications. Every furnishing was in the correct station. They were in the midst of dedicating the Taber-nacle to the Lord. Nobody was inside the *Mishkan*. Suddenly a fireball came from inside the *Mishkan* and ignited the Bronze Altar.

How do we know the sacrifice satisfies the righteous-ness of a holy God? God Himself provides the Ram. By His stripes we are healed. He lights the fire. Jesus is raised from the dead. The seal of God's approval is there for all the world to see.

I love how DeHaan puts it: "Notice carefully, that this fire fell from Heaven, and was not kindled by human hands. Salvation is entirely and exclusively of the Lord (Jonah 2:9). No human effort, no human help, no human con-tribution was made to kindle the fire upon this altar."[1]

Why is it important to note that the fire of the Bronze Altar came from God Himself? _____

_____

The Bronze Altar is where our odyssey to deep intimacy with God begins. It is step one. Without the perfect sacrifice of Jesus, we can go no further. Have you ac-cepted the sacrifice of Jesus on your behalf, dear friend?

If not, by faith pray and freely receive forgiveness from God. Simply say to God, "Thank you, Jesus, for dying for me—the innocent for the guilty. I turn from my sin. I believe in You, Lord. And I receive Your forgiveness. Thank you for my salvation which was purchased at such a great price."

Have you received Jesus as your Savior and Lord? If not, what's stopping you? If you have come to Christ, what does this mean for you? _____

_____

Now that the *penalty* for our sin has been dealt with God's way, we move to step two—the Bronze Basin. God washes us free from the *power* of our sin. Press forward, friend, to station two, the Bronze Basin. Do not make the mistake that so many make and just linger at station one. There is so much more the Lord wants to teach you. If you do not press forward, you will find yourself in an endless cycle of "rededicating" yourself to the Lord again and again, or repeatedly "accepting Christ." Now that you have begun your relationship with Christ, He will show you how to walk in freedom.

By faith what did the Holy Spirit say to you in this section? How will you obey Him? _____

_____

---

1. DeHaan, MR. *The Tabernacle*, Zondervan Publishing House (Grand Rapids, MI), 1955, p. 79.

Chapter 2
The Bronze Basin: Sanctification

"Blessed are the pure in heart for they shall see God" (Matthew 5:8 NKJV).

On our odyssey to deep intimacy with God, the Lord leads us from the Bronze Altar and glorious salvation to supernatural sanctification at the Bronze Basin.

One of the reasons people don't like church is they see the hypocrisy. If people who go to church act just like people who don't go, then what's the point? Jesus saw that coming. He exhorts us to be different. But how do we do that?

For starters, Christians need to take the Bronze Basin seriously. Forgiven does not equal mature. Being set free from the penalty of sin does not mean we are set free from its power. Just because we are free in spirit does not mean we are free in body or soul.

You see, I will be free of you when I am free of me. The reason I am provoked is because I am still provokable. The reason I get offended is because I am still offendable. With Jesus our old cranky self has been crucified, remember? Ever try provoking or offending a dead person? You get no reaction. So in the same way, let us be dead to our old selves. It is Christ who lives in us now.

The Bronze Basin is where we begin to learn how to live free of ourselves. Will we become perfect once we complete this station? No. But we will learn how to control ourselves, how to manage anger, how to mitigate the flesh, and how to flee immorality. It took 40 days to get Israel out of Egypt, but 40 years to get Egypt out of Israel.

Why is the Bronze Basin important? _____

_____

Here's the key passage on the construction and purpose of the Bronze Basin:

"The Lord spoke to Moses: 'You are also to make a large bronze basin with a bronze stand for washing. You are to put it between the tent of meeting and the altar and put water in it, and Aaron and his sons must wash their hands and their feet from it. When they enter the tent of meeting, they must wash with water so that they do not die. Also, when they approach the altar to minister by burning incense as an offering made by fire to the Lord, they must was their hands and their feet so that they do not die. And this will be a perpetual ordinance for them and for their descendants throughout their generations" (Exodus 30:17-21 NET).

The first thing we notice is the lack of instructions on the dimensions of the Basin. The Lord was very precise on the specifications for everything else in the *Mishkan* but when it came to the Bronze Basin, no specifics. Why is that? I like DeHaan's commentary: "There was no command as to its size or dimension. The reason is suggestive. It was limitless in its application"[1]

Unlimited application. At the cross the penalty for all our wrong-doing was wiped away forever. However, we still need to regularly "wash" ourselves of the effects of a fallen world. As long as we live in this fallen world, we will need to ask the Holy Spirit to search our hearts for the imperceptible "bacteria" or "viruses" that lead to moral failure.

In Heaven we see that the Bronze Basin represents a sea of glass. This fits perfectly with why no dimensions are given. For in the spiritual dimension the Bronze Basin is actually an ocean! The Apostle John said, "In front of the throne there was what looked like a sea of glass, clear as crystal" (Revelation 4:6 NIV).

We are the *Mishkan* Temple of the Holy Spirit. The Presence of the Spirit of God within us is a crystal clear ocean, an unlimited supply of righteousness, purity, and grace. It does not mean we can sin all we want. Rather, He designed us with unlimited potential and power to be holy as He is holy! The presence of Christ within us means that His righteousness fills us. His righteousness always trumps our sin as we cry out to Him in confession. Have you ever lost something in the ocean? You'll never find it again. So it is with our sin as we wash in the crystal sea.

Each time the priests entered the Tabernacle they first had to wash their hands and feet. Every time they approached the altar to make an offering before the Lord they first had to wash their hands and feet. How many times did they do this? Was it a dozen times a day? A hundred times a week? The picture we get is that there was a constant need to wash their hands and feet repeatedly, again and again.

Directions for sanctification: lather, rinse, repeat!

We may not know the exact dimensions of the Bronze Basin but it could've been large. It seems like they needed a good supply of water. "Limitless application." It might sound a little OCD, but if it means greater intimacy with a holy God, it is worth being thorough. Remember Jesus said to the Apostles, "Those who have had a bath need only to wash their feet" (John 13:10 NIV).

We had our full bath at the Bronze Altar, now we need to keep our hands and feet clean at the Bronze Basin.

What is significant about no specific dimensions given for the Bronze Basin? _____

_____

The blood of Jesus changed our heart. Now His blood has to course through our entire circulatory system, to our extremities, to our fingertips and toes.

We live in a fallen world but we are no longer fallen. We've been raised up to new life with Jesus. The truth, however, is that the devil and the world have "mentored" us to think and react in certain ways. This is defilement from being in the world. We've been slimed! Sanctification means you no longer live the world's way.

106

This means you are "set apart" from the world and you belong completely to Jesus.

"Do not love *or* cherish the world or the things that are in the world. If anyone loves the world, love for the Father is not in him. For all that is in the world—the lust of the flesh [craving for sensual gratification] and the lust of the eyes [greedy longings of the mind] and the pride of life [assurance in one's own resources or in the stability of earthly things]—these do not come from the Father but are from the world [itself]" (1 John 2:15-16 AMP).

When a Christian still acts like an unbeliever we call that "worldliness." But when a Christian is set apart for God, that is called sanctification or holiness. Are you a worldly Christian or a holy one? Are you still allowing the devil to mentor you in how to think, speak, and act? Or will you let Jesus sanctify you?

What is the Bronze Basin and what is its purpose? Why do we still need sanctification if we were already forgiven at the Bronze Altar? _____

_____

Let's go over some common ways we need sanctification.

Take expectations, for example. Expectations are a two-edged sword. On the one hand we can have a great sense of expectancy about what God is going to do. He is the God for whom nothing is impossible. On the other hand when things don't go the way we *expect*, we can be disappointed. And it seems the greater the expectation the greater the disappointment. This can lead to people getting upset. If we do not know how to manage our emotions, this can be extremely disruptive in Church. This is why we need the Bronze Basin.

Sometimes when we hear about somebody getting healed but it doesn't happen the exact same way to us, we can be disappointed. We hear how Jesus changes lives, but if our life doesn't change the same way, "flat tire!"

This leads some to say that they tried Christianity but it didn't work for them. The Lord, however, knows exactly what He's doing. He didn't save us so He could become our genie in a lamp. He is taking us on a journey to deeper intimacy with Him. And that means our character needs to change. Our minds need to be renewed. At the Bronze Basin the Spirit of Jesus transforms our character.

Remember our spirit is totally brand new but our soul still has issues. Jesus has given us a complete spiritual blood transfusion. We are not the same person we were before because spiritually we have a new relationship with God. However, our soul still has issues. Now the Holy Spirit, who is now one with our spirit, needs to wash over our soul.

When we first come from the world, we generally think everything is about us. We expect the Church to meet our expectations. We expect the pastor to be there for us. We expect God to be a certain way.

Contrary to popular belief, at the heart of Satanism is not the worship of Satan but the worship of self. I am not saying self-centered people are Satanists. But when we live primarily for self, that is the central tenet of the black church.

God takes us on a journey from being self-centered to being God-centered. We go from being all about us to all about Him. We die to our expectations. We pray "Thy Kingdom come, Thy will be done," not *my* kingdom come, *my* will be done. We come humbly before the Father who knows what we need before we ask Him. We ask the Spirit to help us pray because we don't really know what to pray for. When we come out of the world, our expectations become sanctified. How? At the Bronze Basin the Lord washes us our minds with His Word and sanctifies our hearts by His Spirit.

In what ways do our expectations need sanctification? _

_____

Now let's address emotional health and wholeness. Families these days go through so many things that can have a devastating impact on children—divorce, sexual abuse, emotional abuse, physical abuse, death of a family member, drug abuse, and alcoholism. The list is endless. These may open a door for a host of emotional issues—rejection, abandonment, insecurity, inferiority, scarcity, and shame. Another endless list.

At the heart of this is what can be called an "orphan soul." Shortly before His death, Jesus said to His Apostles, "I will not leave you as orphans; I will come to you" (John 14:18 NASB). Jesus knew His disciples would feel abandoned like orphans after witnessing His traumatic execution. They had placed all their hopes in Him, left their homes and families to follow Him. Now they would eyewitness the horrific death of their leader. It would be perfectly natural for them to feel abandoned like an orphan. In the same way it is perfectly natural for people to feel deep insecurity and abandonment after what they've gone through in the past.

Sometimes life treats you like a baby treats a diaper.

At the Bronze Basin, however, we learn the key to emotional health and wholeness—His Presence! When Jesus came to the Temple in Jerusalem, He found it had become a den of thieves. So he cleaned them out with extreme prejudice. That's what you call zeal for God's house! He is no less zealous to clean out your Temple, friend. Would you allow Him to overturn the money-changers in your heart?

How will you allow the Lord to clean our your Temple?

_____

_____

No matter what happens in life, Jesus will never leave us or forsake us. His Spirit comes to us at the Bronze Basin to say, "You've got this, because I've got you." He does not promise us that there won't be diaper days. In fact, He says the exact opposite: "Here on Earth you will have many trials and sorrows. (Diaper days!) But take heart, because I have overcome the world." (John 16:33 NLT). At the Bronze Basin we learn to return to Him again and again each time we are slimed by the world. On this side of Heaven, our goal is not a trouble-free life, but rather a life of freedom. Freedom doesn't come from asking God to take away our problems but from experiencing the power of God to overcome our problems.

In Hawaii we do our baptisms at the ocean. It is perhaps

the most beautiful setting in all the world for baptism—
majestic mountains, blue sky touching the horizon, and
the vast Pacific Ocean.

I remind our people, "Have you ever lost anything in the
ocean?" My son, Caleb, had a GoPro that he had
strapped to his hand. It was a Hero 3 Black Edition.
This GoPro was sweet. But a wave hit it and knocked it
out of his hand. You would think it would be really easy
to find since he was right by where it came off. No such
luck. Goodbye GoPro. Forever. It is now taking endless
video of Davey Jones' locker. And so it is with our sin
when we wash in the crystal sea of the Spirit. We just
need to remember that the next time we get slimed.
Lather, rinse, repeat.

By faith what did the Holy Spirit say to you in this
section? How will you obey Him? _____

_____

1. DeHaan, MR. *The Tabernacle*, Zondervan Publishing
House (Grand Rapids, MI), 1955, pp. 86-87.

Part 2

The Holy Place

EQUIP

The Holy Place

EQUIP

From the Outer Court you face west to see the entrance to the Temple. The soft glow of candlelight emanates from the opening. Inside you hear the voices of your brothers and sisters in Christ—the royal priesthood of believers. As you enter you are greeted by their smiling faces and warm embraces. God is love. God is love in a Triune family. You immediately detect God's Manifest Presence in the love of those who are filled with His Spirit.

In this room you realize that the furnishings are no longer bronze. They are gold. There is a Golden Table on the north side of the room, a Golden Lamp to the south, and directly ahead of you, a Golden Altar.

The Holy Place is where you learn to experience God's Presence in Christian friendship. At each of these stations are golden lessons on how to see God in those who are created in His image. Equally important, you will learn how others can see the image of God in you.

The Holy Place is where God's people are equipped to

love one another as Jesus loved them. The command has been updated from "as you love yourself" to "as Jesus loved you." It is an awesome and glorious thing to be saved by Jesus, but a key test of your salvation is will you die to yourself for the sake of others as Jesus died for you.

The Master said, "A new commandment I give to you, that you love one another, even as I have loved you, that you also love one another. By this all men will know that you are My disciples, if you have love for one another" (John 13:34-35 cf. 15:12).

There is a Holy Place within you, dear friend. Here, God encounters you through the love of others and *your* love *for* others. This is called fellowship.

Not everything people say in fellowship is from the Lord. Not everything the pastor teaches is from the Lord. But more frequently than you imagine, God speaks to you through imperfect human beings. By the instruction and inner witness of the Holy Spirit, you learn to tell the difference between His voice and theirs. This is not an easy task when He might use their shrill tones and poorly chosen words to convey His message.

The Good Shepherd, however, guarantees that you will recognize His voice amidst a myriad of voices. Welcome to the Holy Place where you learn to experience His Presence in fellowship with the Body of Christ.

Why do you think God designed you with a Holy Place? _____

_____

Chapter 3
The Golden Table of Bread: Scripture

To have a place at the Lord's Table means we belong, we are family. The deepest longing of the human heart is to belong. We long to belong.

Jesus said, "Behold, I stand at the door and knock; if anyone hears My voice and opens the door, I will come in to him and *will dine with him* (italics mine), and he with Me" (Revelation 3:20 NASB).

This is such a beautiful picture of the Lord's heart for intimate fellowship with us. The most precious times of friendship happen when we get together and eat. Sitting around the table together is a classic picture of precious friendship whether it is families gathering for Thanksgiving, friends going out for a bite, couples on a date for dinner and a movie, or a wedding reception.

In Church Jesus is the center of our fellowship with one another. Jesus knocks on our door and calls out to us, "Let's get together! You have a place at My table."

How does sitting at the Lord's Table give us a picture of fellowship with Jesus? _____

_____

The Table of Bread raises three questions about our intimate fellowship with the Lord: What is the foundation of our fellowship with Him (past)? What is our (present) focus? And what is the (future) of our fellowship with the Lord?

For many people bread is something you eat with peanut butter and jelly. But for Christians and Jews bread evokes powerful imagery of the supernatural salvation of God throughout biblical history.

Through Moses God miraculously gave His people manna in the wilderness. Through Joseph's Egyptian granaries God saved His people and countless others from famine. On Passover when the angel of death *passed over* the Hebrews in Egypt, they ate bread. Elijah and Elisha both had amazing bread miracles.

In the Bible what powerful imagery does "bread" evoke? _____

_____

The ultimate, supreme authority on bread and the Bible, however, is of course Jesus. Jesus was born in Bethlehem, "house of bread." Fully aware of what bread means to His people, Jesus identifies Himself as the Bread of Life (John 6:35). In John 6 Jesus gives such an advanced teaching about Himself being the Bread of Life that He loses thousands of followers except for the Twelve. Why did the crowd abandon Him? And more importantly why did the Apostles stay?

Let's summarize what happens. In John 6 Jesus miraculously feeds the 5,000 by multiplying five loaves and two fish. The people are so blown away by this they want to draft Him to be their king. When they realize that Jesus also walked on the water, their zeal to crown Him king intensifies. Jesus refuses this kind of political power. It is not the kind of community transformation He has in mind. Later, He would accept a crown of thorns instead.

So at what point does the crowd turn against Him? Was it his confusing reference to cannibalism? "Whoever eats my flesh and drinks my blood remains in me, and I in them" (John 6:56 NIV). That certainly put a crimp in their coronation plans. Here's the last thing Jesus said before the crowd left:

"Does this offend you? Then what if you see the Son of Man ascend to where he was before! The Spirit gives life; the flesh counts for nothing. The words I have spoken to you—they are full of the Spirit and life. Yet there are some of you who do not believe...This is why I told you that no one can come to me unless the Father has enabled them" (John 6:62-65 NASB).

After this John writes, "From this time many of his disciples turned back and no longer followed him" (John 6:66 NIV). I always thought it was interesting that this occurred at verse 666. After everybody was gone Jesus turned to the Apostles and asked, "You do not want to leave too, do you?" Speaking for the Twelve, Simon Peter responded, "Lord, to whom shall we go? You have the words of eternal life. We have come to believe and to know that you are the Holy One of God" (John 6:68-69 NIV).

So what just happened? How did Jesus go from a mega church of over 5,000 back down to twelve guys?

In hindsight we now see that Jesus was prophesying about how His death on the Cross would make possible the oneness that He spoke of. By His blood we remain in Him and He in us. The analogy of "eating" is really quite profound. If you were to actually eat a peanut butter and jelly sandwich, an hour from now you wouldn't point to your arm and say, "Here's the sandwich I ate earlier." Why? The reason is the sandwich has been absorbed into your whole being. You and the sandwich have become one.

In the same way Jesus, the Bread of Life, once "eaten" dwells in our whole being. This is amazing Temple language! But at this point in their spiritual journey most of the believers had no way of latching on to what Jesus was saying. All they knew was that Jesus was a miracle worker, and if they crowned Him king maybe He would keep feeding them free food.

The Apostles on the other hand, Simon Peter specifically, could discern the "deep magic." They knew He was talking about something far more profound than political power or a lifetime of free meals. Listen again to what Peter said: "Lord, to whom shall we go? You have the words of eternal life. We have come to believe and to know that you are the Holy One of God" (John 6:68-69 NIV).

As far as Peter was concerned, they had come to the end of their search. In Jesus they had encountered the Living Bread of Heaven in the flesh. They knew their ancestors who ate the original bread from Heaven—manna—eventually died. But in Jesus they had met the One who sent the manna! They had met the Bread of Heaven Himself who sent the bread from Heaven.

And how were they to "eat" this bread exactly? The words of Jesus are the Bread. Peter said, "You have the words of eternal life." Jesus said that His words are Spirit and life.

Let's put it all together: Jesus = Bread of Life = the Living Word = Spirit and Life.

At the Last Supper Jesus reminded them of this teaching: "This bread is My body." Jesus was saying, "Remember how Joseph saved our people with his vast stockpiles of grain? That was Me. And remember how manna came from Heaven to save Moses and our people? That was Me too. And remember how you were breaking bread in your homes in Egypt as the angel of death passed over you because of the lamb's blood on your doorposts? Yes, me again. Now you are about to behold My *ultimate* act of salvation for all mankind!"

At the Last Supper Jesus answers the question: What is the foundation of our fellowship with God? How is it that we get to experience such intimacy with God? The Cross is the reason.

The Cross is Christ's magnum opus, His greatest work, His masterpiece.

The bread is unleavened—pure. It is made of crushed wheat, just as His body would be crushed. The wine— crushed grapes—is His blood. Our fellowship with a holy God came at such a price! But He was willing to pay it. It was paid in total. Our sin totally destroyed our fellowship with God. The Cross totally restored it. The death sentence for our sin was cast upon Jesus. The Innocent dies for the guilty. Once again the specter of death would *pass over* those marked by the blood of the Lamb on the doorpost of their heart. The resurrection is proof of the Father's approval. At the Table of Bread we remember this supreme act of love that established the foundation of our fellowship with God. Nothing can or should be added to it. It is finished.

How does the Cross lay the foundation for our fellowship with God ? _____

_____

If the Cross established our fellowship with God in the past, what should our focus be in the present? In the Holy Place, the Bread on the Table represents His Presence in our fellowship now. It is also called "Showbread," bread that *shows* us God's Presence. Jesus promised, "I will not leave you as orphans. I will come to you" (John 14:18 NASB). Today our resurrected, ascended Lord is with us as the Presence of the Holy Spirit within us. Therefore, our present focus in fellowship is His Manifest Presence.

Now watch this: Jesus, the Bread of Life, says, "Man shall not live on bread alone, but on every word that comes from the mouth of God" (Matthew 4:4 NIV Cf. Deuteronomy 8:3). Jesus contends that our true need is not physical but Spiritual, not just mere bread but His Word. Jesus is the embodiment of the Word of God in human form. "And the Word became flesh and dwelt (or tabernacled) among us" (John 1:14). Jesus is the Living

Word of God who therefore gives us the true Bread of Life, the Manifest Presence of God dwelling within us. Remember Jesus is the Bread which is His Word which is the Spirit. This is who dwells within us. That's an awesome perspective on the *Mishkan* Temple right there!

On our odyssey to intimacy with God, our commitment to Scripture, therefore, is non-negotiable.

At the Golden Table of Bread we learn how to accurately interpret the Bible.

Hermeneutics is the discipline of accurate interpretation of the Bible. Sometimes we hear, "Well, I have a different interpretation of the Bible." Did you know there is only one correct interpretation of Scripture? There are unlimited applications but only one interpretation. All Scripture is inspired by God, but the Lord worked through 40 human authors to give us the Bible. Each human author wrote in a unique moment in history. Knowing the historical background, the issue he was addressing, whom he was addressing, and special circumstances of the author is called *context*. When we know the context we can better understand the one thing the author was trying to communicate. But take his words out of context, and we can make the Bible say just about anything we want it to say. And that's where cults come from.

Let's say we're driving on a country road in the continental US, but since I'm from Hawaii I need directions. So I pull into a gas station to ask for help. The guy tells me, "Go down this road then *bear* right." In Hawaii we don't talk funny like that. So as we're driving my son yells out, "Look, dad, there's a bear!" "Where, son? Where's the bear?" I ask. "On the right!" he says, "Bear right!" So I turn right. What just happened? I got more lost! Why? I didn't understand the *context* of that man's use of the word "bear." In the same way, if we don't understand the context of Scripture, we will get lost reading the Bible.

However, our approach to the written word must not be merely grammatical. It must lead us to Spiritual food, the Living Word. If our time in the Word is boring and stale, then perhaps we did not connect with the Living Word. If it is merely an academic exercise we did not accomplish the true purpose for studying the Scripture. By faith our time in the Word must eventually lead to a divine encounter—a moment where we sense the Spirit speaking to us.

Why is it so important that Christians handle accurately the Word of God? _____

_____

This is that moment in our study of Scripture when we know in our heart and mind that God is speaking to us. A passage becomes highlighted to us. A verse written thousands of years ago hits us with a fresh relevance. We will never be transformed by taking principles from the bible and applying them to our lives. We are transformed when we hear the voice of God and respond in obedience. The written Word leads us to the Living Word.

Man shall not live by bread alone but by the Living Word of the Spirit in the Holy Scriptures.

As *Mishkan* Temples, there is a Table of Bread within us. This is where we encounter the Presence of God in fellowship with other Christians through the Word of the Spirit. How many times have you heard someone say, "Wow, today's message was exactly what I needed to hear!"

Consider for a moment how powerful and Spiritual the Word is. A preacher speaks the Word. It travels through the airwaves to a person's ears. Then the person's mind deciphers the message. By Divine orchestration the biblical principle has something to do with what is going on in the person's life. The Word might give the person truth that dispels a lie, conviction to live differently, or new hope to carry on. This is incredibly Spiritual!

It is the power of the Spirit at work to transform us. God is speaking to us through the Word of the Spirit. We do not take biblical principles and apply them in our own strength. This will lead to legalism and death. We will eventually set the Bible aside in frustration. Instead, live in response to what the *Spirit* is saying to us in His Word. This is what we focus on.

How does our present focus on the Word of the Spirit transform our experience in fellowship? _____

_____

At the Table of Bread our past foundation is the Cross and our present focus is the Word of the Spirit. Now we must ask, "Where is Jesus taking us in the future?"

As He was celebrating the Passover with His disciples at

the Last Supper, three times Jesus alluded to a future time where He would sit at Table with us. Jesus prophesied a time when the Kingdom of God would come and He would eat and drink with the disciples once again. Jesus knew that His death would make this future possible. And He longed for it.

Jesus said to them, "I have earnestly desired to eat this Passover with you before I suffer; for I say to you, I shall never again eat it until it is fulfilled in the kingdom of God" (Luke 22:15-16 NASB).

Then Jesus took the cup, gave thanks, and said, "I will not drink of the fruit of the vine from now on until the kingdom of God comes" (Luke 22:18 NASB).

A third time Jesus said, "Just as My Father has granted Me a kingdom, I grant you that you may eat and drink at My Table in My kingdom, and you will sit on thrones judging the twelve tribes of Israel" (Luke 22:29-30 NASB).

In this present age the world treats Christians as they treated the Lord. We long for the coming of the Kingdom in its fullness where we will be reunited with the Master. The temporary tribulations of this life pale in comparison with the joy of sitting at the Lord's Table in His eternal Kingdom.

Whatever hardship or persecution you face, take heart, dear friend. The Earth is about to give way to an entirely new matrix beyond mortal imagination. For God will establish His Kingdom on Earth as it is in Heaven. This old world is going away. And because of our fellowship with the King of Heaven, we have reservations already set to sit at His Table in the new age to come. Can't wait for that!

How does the fact that we have reserved seats at the Lord's Table in the future affect our experience of Christian fellowship today? _____

_____

Can you see now how awesome it is to have Jesus at the center of our fellowship with one another? With Jesus at the center, we become the Church anchored to God's Word and led by His Spirit. Without Jesus at the center, we deform into a man-centered church full of human agendas.

The Table of Bread prompts us to remember the past, that the foundation of our fellowship with Jesus is the Cross. Today the Table of Bread is where we encounter the Manifest Presence of the Spirit of Jesus in the breaking of the Bread of Life—the Living Word of God. Finally, the Table of Bread assures us that for all time we will have a place at the Table of the Lord, that we belong to His family forever. Hallelujah!

By faith what did the Holy Spirit say to you in this section? How will you obey Him? _____

_____

Chapter 4
The Golden Lamp: Testimony

As soon as I became a Christian in 1975 I was so radically touched by the Holy Spirit that I immediately began sharing Jesus with my family. My sister and three brothers came to Jesus immediately, the first time I shared with them. But my parents were steeped in Catholicism, so it took them 10 years to see that this was not just a "religious phase" their children were going through. Eventually they also gave their hearts to the Lord.

Uncles, aunties, cousins, nephews, and nieces all came to Jesus. No one told me I was supposed to do this. I was just overwhelmed with compassion for them to know Jesus as I did. At first I didn't know any "Gospel presentations." Later I would learn the Roman Road, Steps to Peace with God, the Bridge Illustration, etc. But in the beginning I simply shared what the Lord did in my own life—what I was like before Jesus, how I met Him, and how He changed me.

That's called a testimony.

Every follower of Jesus has a testimony. Basically, it's a

story of "before and after." What was your life like be-fore Jesus? How did you meet Jesus? What is your life like now as a follower of Christ? Your testimony is the end result of your encounter of Jesus at the Golden Lamp. The ministry you serve in is the vehicle through which the light of your testimony shines.

What is a testimony and how is it related to ministry? __

_____

Let us first rewind the tape to understand the origin and deeper meaning of the Golden Lamp.

On the south side of the Holy Place is the Golden Lamp (Exodus 25:31; 37:17). It is called the Menorah. This seven-branched candelabrum is the sacred symbol of the State of Israel. What is its significance? The heart of the Golden Lamp can be found in a mystical encounter the prophet Zechariah had with an angel of the Lord.

"And the angel who talked with me came again and awakened me, like a man who is wakened out of his sleep. And said to me, 'What do you see?' I said, 'I see, and behold, a lampstand all of gold, with its bowl [for oil] on the top of it and its seven lamps on it, and [there are] seven pipes to each of the seven lamps which are upon the top of it'" (Zechariah 4:1-2 AMP).

Judging from the description, the angel is clearly show-ing Zechariah a vision of a Menorah. But it seems to have some interesting modifications—a catchment for oil and a system of pipes. What is going on here?

"And there are two olive trees by it, one upon the right side of the bowl and the other upon the left side of it [feeding it continuously with oil]. So I asked the angel who talked with me, What are these, my lord? Then the angel who talked with me answered me, Do you not know what these are? And I said, No, my lord" (Zechariah 4:3-5 AMP).

The Menorah uses olive oil as fuel for its light. Zechariah sees two olive trees on each side providing a continuous supply of oil through the pipe system. What happens next is absolutely amazing:

"Then he said to me, 'This [addition of the bowl to the candlestick, causing it to yield a ceaseless supply of oil from the olive trees] is the word of the Lord to Zerubbabel, saying, "Not by might, nor by power, but by My Spirit [of Whom the oil is a symbol], says the Lord of hosts""" (Zechariah 4:6 AMP).

Wow! Did you catch that? The oil represents none other than the Spirit of the Lord! The power to be a light to the nations does not originate from ourselves. It is not by our own might or power that we serve God, but by the Spirit of the Lord.

Israel has chosen as its national symbol a vision that would serve as a perpetual reminder to them that the source of their strength is never in themselves but rather in the Spirit of the Lord.

Throughout the history of the people of God, where does their help come from? The Spirit of the Lord!

Like the burning bush of Moses that was not consumed, the fuel for our fire originates from a supernatural source.

As the Church shines with the light of its testimony, our dependence is not in our own power, but rather the continuous, ceaseless flow of power from the Spirit.

What is the Golden Lamp and why is it significant? ____

The amazing Jewish story of Hanukah or Chanukah (which means "dedication") is a powerful testimony of the Golden Lamp. Jesus celebrated Chanukah (John 10:22). What is Hanukah about? The year was 167 BC. The mad and ruthless Syrian-Greek king Antiochus Epiphanes IV oppressed the Jews with a terrible persecution. He desecrated the Temple by placing a pagan statue of Zeus inside it and sacrificing a pig on the altar —acts so abominable some believe this was the abomination of desolation that Daniel spoke of. The very existence of the Jewish nation was on the line.

In the midst of this darkness a hero arose. Judah Maccabee (known as the "Hammer") was from the town of Modein. His father, Mattityahu, began a revolution that cast off their Hellenistic oppressors. Against all odds they took on the superpower of the day and won. They went from desecration to revolution to dedication. They eradicated the pagan idols and *rededicated* the Temple and themselves to the Lord. This was yet another Esther-like moment in Jewish history. The Jewish faith and culture were on the brink of extinction. Without it we could not have Christmas as we know it. How did it happen? "Not by might nor by power, but by My Spirit."

During the desecration, legend has it that no one could refill the Menorah with oil to keep the eternal fire lit.

Only one day of fuel remained. But mysteriously the Menorah remained lit for eight days, enough time to produce more oil. "Not by might, nor by power, but by My Spirit."

To this day around November or December, Jews everywhere celebrate Chanukah. They use a special Menorah with nine branches instead of seven so that a candle could be lit to commemorate each of the eight miraculous days.

How does the story of Chanukah illustrate the meaning of "not by might nor by power but by My Spirit?" _____

_____

The Golden Lamp is the fourth station on our odyssey to Temple His Spirit. When the Apostle John received the Revelation from Jesus, we learned what the Lamp represented in the spiritual dimension: "The seven lampstands are the seven churches" (Revelation 1:20 NIV). The meaning is straight forward: The Spirit of Jesus abides in the Church. He is the Light. We are His lampstand. The Church is the hope of the world insofar as a lampstand houses a light bulb. This is how Jesus has chosen to reveal Himself to the world today.

As the *Mishkan* Temple of the Holy Spirit, there is a Golden Lamp within you. Your testimony is a light that radiates from you, testifying to the world of the love of God.

Jesus said of Himself, "I am the Light of the world" (John 8:12). Then He told His disciples, "You are the light of the world" (Matthew 5:14). Then He urged us to place our lamps on a stand so people can see our good works and give glory to the Father.

Once we encounter Jesus His marvelous light shines forth from our lives. And He wants the world to see His Light so He can be glorified and the world can be transformed.

I am writing this to you from Hawaii, the remotest spot on Earth from Jerusalem. Today one-third of the world's population worships at the feet of Jesus. Jesus is the most influential person who ever lived. And the Bible is the number one best seller of all time. How did this happen? The Church has been shining the Light of Jesus to the world!

The heart of God, however, is not content with one-third of the people of the Earth. He wants to reach out to every unsaved, unchurched person on the planet. His eye is not just on the one-third who are already in Church, but on the two-thirds of the world who are not. Jesus said if He had 100 sheep and lost one, He would leave the 99 to search for the one.

In the story of the prodigal son, I am struck by Jesus' attention to detail: "So he got up and went to his father. But while he was still a long way from home his father saw him, and his heart went out to him; he ran and hugged his son and kissed him" (Luke 15:20 NET). The One who knew the Father better than anyone tells us how the Father sees us coming from a long way off, gets up, and starts running toward us! And when He gets to us, get ready for all the hugs and kisses. Every person is valuable like that to God.

The disciples, filled with the Spirit, caught the heart of God. Peter said that the Lord is "not willing that one should perish, but that all should come to repentance" (2 Peter 3:9). Paul said that God wants "all people to be saved and to come to a knowledge of the truth" (1 Tim. 2:4). All those who know God intimately have this same compassion for people.

Don't forget the Lord says, "Not by might, nor by power, but by My Spirit." How does this happen in our lives today? The Holy Spirit empowers us to bear the fruit of the Spirit which is the character of Jesus (Galatians 5:22-23). The Holy Spirit also activates the gifts of the Spirit which are the abilities of Jesus (1 Corinthians 12; Romans 12; Ephesians 4). The Holy Spirit empowers us to be His witnesses which is the mission of Jesus (Acts 1:8). Therefore, when we see fruit, gifts, and witnessing occur in our lives, that is not our own power. That's the Holy Spirit!

What are three ways the Holy Spirit empowers us to reach the lost? _____

_____

The heart to "seek and to save that which was lost" has not changed. But after 40 years of harvesting I would like to highlight three lessons on how to be as effective as possible in the field:

(1) Continue to make your own personal impact in evangelism, (2) work together as a ministry team, and (3) follow the leadership of the Holy Spirit.

Without question every individual Christian is part of an intricate local and global organism with many essential parts all necessary to accomplish the mission. However,

I urge you to never stop personally leading people to Jesus! It is easy for leaders to fall into the trap of thinking, "My job is to equip others to evangelize" and not do it ourselves.

In my zeal to be an effective equipper I found myself pursuing, training, and deploying as many leaders as I could. So we met for discipleship early in morning, went to conferences together, then started doing our own conferences. Before long I found myself surrounded only by Christians! I didn't have any unsaved friends. I rarely even spoke to unchurched people. What's worse it seemed like all the Christians I knew also hung out mostly with other Christians. So *they* weren't reaching out to anyone either!

That's when I felt like the Holy Spirit spoke to me. In effect He said something like, "What happened to you? You used to have such a heart for the lost. Now you leave it to others to reach them while you sit in your Christian ivory tower." Ouch. So I inquired of the Lord how to break out of the Christian rut I was in.

The Lord highlighted a guy to me named Ron who had started coming to Church. Ron was on fire for Jesus and just won an election to City Council. I simply asked him if we could pray together with his staff in his office at City Hall once a week. It was a totally voluntary meeting before the work day. Ron thought it was a great idea! Long story short I started to make friends with his staff at City Hall and began sharing Christ with those who didn't know Him. Two people and their spouses came to Jesus! Ron and those who were already believers were super encouraged. It was awesome to lead people to Christ one on one again. After years of speaking to crowds and giving altar calls, there was something wonderfully refreshing about doing this again. Has the Lord given you an open door or strategy to personally lead people to Jesus? Go for it! If not, ask the Lord to lead you. It is so much fun!

List the name of someone you could personally lead to Jesus. _____

_____

Now let's address the second thing to make you extremely effective: Work as a team. As I said earlier, you're not alone. You don't have to work alone. And God never intended you to. Wayne Cordeiro, the spiritual father of the New Hope movement, already wrote the best thing ever written on ministry teamwork in his book, *Doing Church As Team.* If you haven't read it yet, get it now! I can't improve on anything he said in that amazing book. It defined the New Hope movement for all of us. That said, allow me to encourage you as Wayne does to go on a journey to discover, develop, and deploy your spiritual gift mix.

God said to Jeremiah, "Before I formed you in the womb I knew you, and before you were born I consecrated you; I have appointed you a prophet to the nations" (Jeremiah 1:5 NASB). This means that God had a purpose in mind *first* and then He created you. Have you ever asked yourself, "How can God *know* Jeremiah before Jeremiah was conceived in his mother's womb?" The answer is God *thought* of Jeremiah before Jeremiah came into existence. God *predesigned* Jeremiah before He created him. Jeremiah was *preconceived* by God before he was *conceived.* God first thought to Himself, "I need a prophet to the nations." Then the second thing He did was design a Jeremiah in his mother's womb.

There is *something* God wants to accomplish and then He creates *someone* to do it. I will return to this idea in chapter seven. For now you just need to know there is nothing random about you. Your passions, gifts, talents, skills, experiences (good and bad)—everything about you!—can be redeemed to be a light to others. Moreover, because you are part of a team, you don't need to feel like it's up to you to do everything. Just go on that journey to discover how God designed you and join the appropriate ministry team in Church. And if there is no ministry team that seems to match what God designed you for, ask your pastor to help you create one! It is possible that God may want to birth a new ministry through you.

What ministry has the Holy Spirit gifted you to do? ____

_____

Finally, let's contend for following the leadership of the Holy Spirit. Don't forget that Jesus said, "I am with you always to the very end of the age" (Matthew 28:20 NIV). We can count on the Lord to personally lead us and guide us. Even if something seems like "common sense," just make it a habit to take it to prayer first and ask the Lord. Don't use this as an excuse to defy your pastor! Often pastors are not aware of everything you are doing. If your pastor asks you to serve in a ministry but you're already serving in two others, it is *not* defiance to share that with him. On the other hand, if your pastor asks you to serve and you're not serving anywhere else, give it your best shot. That's why God gives us pastors! They equip us and shepherd us to do God's will. Together with your pastor ask God for His will in your life.

In what current area of ministry do you need the leading of the Holy Spirit? _____

_____

As a *Mishkan* Temple of the Spirit, there is a Golden Lamp within you—a divine light that shines in a dark world. There is no one else that has the same story or experience as you on how they encountered Jesus. Can you articulate your story? If you don't tell it, we would all be the poorer for it. There is no one else that has your unique spiritual gifts and abilities. Do you know your spiritual gifts? If you don't deploy them, the rest of the Church will be that much less effective. The way God speaks to you is uniquely personal. The purpose for which He created you is equally special. Do you know what He designed you to accomplish for Him? At the Golden Lamp you learn how to love, live, and serve not by your own might or power but by the power of the Spirit who dwells within you.

From Filipino Playboy to Man of God
Mike Palompo's Testimony

In the summer of 1975, there once was a 17-year-old kid named Mike Palompo with a bright future. He was the newly elected student body president of Radford High School about to go into his senior year. He showed a lot of promise, but considered himself the "dumb Asian" because he was only ranked 16th in his class of 600 students. That's because he was always "looking for love in all the wrong places." He was a Filipino playboy always getting his heart broken. He fully believed, "Men aren't born monogamous." You see, he may have looked good on the outside but on the inside he was empty, dark, and lived for one main purpose—himself. But all that was about to change.

His best friend, Mark Olmos, came up to him the night of July 17, 1975 and said, "Mike, you need to talk to Amanda!" Amanda was a new friend visiting from the Big Island. She was cute, but she was always going around saying "praise the Lord" this and "praise the Lord" that. Weird. But hey, she was cute. Mark seemed unusually adamant. "Talk to her about what?" Mike asked. "You just need to talk to her!" The next night Mike, Mark, Amanda, and some other friends went to the Honolulu Concert Hall to listen to Hal Lindsey, author of *The Late*

Great Planet Earth. It was a book that all their friends on campus were reading. So they went to hear the man who claimed the end of the world was about to happen. At the end of his talk, Hal invited people to come forward to receive Christ. Mike and friends were sitting way in the back of the auditorium. Never having seen anything like this before, Mike just sat there watching the stage fill up with people.

Later that same night all the friends hung out in a house in Foster Village to play trumps, a card game. In the middle of a hand, Amanda turned to Mike and said, "Did you want to talk to me about something?" "Huh? No, not really," Mike said, continuing to play. Five minutes later Amanda grabbed Mike by the wrist and took him into the next room. "What's going on?" he thought to himself. Sitting on the couch in the next room, Amanda asked, "What did you think of what Hal Lindsey said tonight?" "I don't know. It might be true," Mike responded. "Well, I believe with all my heart that Jesus will return to Earth one day, and we need to be ready," Amanda said.

She then began to tell Mike about how much God loved him, that the reason Jesus died on the cross was to pay the penalty for his sin once and for all. Growing up Catholic Mike knew about Jesus dying on the cross but never understood why. That night Amanda's words came piercing through his heart with a clarity he never had before. "Of course!" he realized. "Jesus died to pay the penalty for *my* sin *once and for all.*" All the years of going to church, taking communion, confessing sin, praying penance, and performing other religious duties could never take away sin. Jesus died once and for all for the sin of mankind and then offers His forgiveness as a free gift. Only by His grace can we be saved!

"Do you want to receive Jesus into your heart tonight, Mike?" Amanda asked. "Yes." Then repeat this prayer after me: "Lord Jesus, thank you for dying for me. Thank you for paying the price for my sin on the cross once and for all. I have sinned, but now I turn away from my past life. And I receive your forgiveness! Come into my heart, Lord, and I will follow You for the rest of my life. Amen."

Mike had an amazing encounter with the Lord that night that transformed his life forever. He was set free from sin. He honestly believed he would never sin again, he felt so free. (Later he realized that transformation happened over a lifetime.) But God's unconditional love for him didn't depend on his perfection. It was like a heavy weight was lifted off his shoulders. That night he experienced an immediate emotional healing. From a low-grade depression he was instantly filled with overflowing joy in his new relationship with Christ. The darkness gave way to a new light that filled his soul. He went from Filipino playboy to man of God.

Over time Mike underwent perhaps the most amazing transformation of his life—from "playing the field" to a devoted husband! He married Mona Waki in 1983, and they've been married ever since. It all began that Friday night, July 18, 1975, 11:30 PM.

Turns out the reason Mark was so insistent that Mike talk to Amanda was because Amanda had led Mark to Christ the day before on July 17. They had come to Christ within a day of each other! And this was the beginning of a lifelong friendship.

There was no Christian Club at Radford High School at

the time, so they pioneered one. It was called the John 14:6 Club. They learned guitar so they could lead worship. And they started studying the Bible. Often whatever they just learned was what they discussed in the club. And they kept sharing Jesus with as many friends as possible. Nobody told Mike that missionary dating was unwise, so he did that too. At least now he was dating for a redemptive purpose. His new philosophy was "flirt to convert." (As you can see he still lacked a lot of wisdom.)

Eventually, the John 14:6 Club became the Radford Campus Life Club. After graduating from high school and college, Mark and Mike served Jesus together as full-time Campus Life Directors with Hawaii Youth For Christ. They were each other's best man on their wedding days. Mike even named his firstborn son Mark after his best friend. After Youth For Christ, the Lord led each of them into Church ministry. Pastor Mark planted Faith Christian Fellowship and Pastor Mike planted New Hope Central Oahu. Although they live in different states now, they continue to be the best of friends and serve Jesus with all their hearts.

Special Exercise
Write Your Personal Testimony

Now we'll have you write down *your* testimony so you can share it clearly with others.

1. **Before** you came to Christ, what were you like? What were your attitudes like? Who did you hang out with? What were you living for? What were your biggest struggles?

2. How did you become a Christian? What was the date? What was the event? Who led you to Christ?

3. **After** becoming a Christian, what are the most significant ways your life has changed?

Chapter 5
The Golden Altar of Incense: Prayer

When I was in sixth grade I played for my school basketball team, the St. Andrew Spartans. I remember that I used to kneel by my bedside the night before a game with my arms outstretched pleading with God to help me score points for the team. I thought that the longer I kept my arms up the more I proved to God how sincere I was. So I kept my arms up until they hurt so bad I couldn't hold them up anymore. The next day my arms were so sore I couldn't score! Obviously, I didn't know how to pray. Even after giving my heart to Christ, my prayer life still consisted of "informing" God of what I thought needed to happen.

It is no wonder that the final station just outside the Holy of Holies deals with our prayer lives. How we pray says a lot about how we see God and how we relate to Him.

In contrast with my younger self, how would you describe the prayer life of Jesus? Jesus was the most amazing Person who ever lived. Peerless character. Authoritative teaching. Miraculous ministry. Mass Evangelism. Effective discipleship. But what was the key to His life and ministry? The answer: His prayer life. He was the perfect example of how a human being, a child of God prays to know Abba's will. So the million dollar question is "what was His prayer life like exactly?"

In his book *Listening to the God Who Speaks*, Klaus Bockmuehl calls Jesus the "Great Listener." And that's the key. Instead of *informing* God of what needed to be done, Jesus spent more time *being informed*. And then He stepped out in perfect submission and obedience. Once in the Garden of Gethsemane just before His crucifixion, He expressed His human heart: "Take this cup from Me." But in the same breath He prayed, "Yet not My will but Yours be done." Of course He didn't want to die, but He knew the cross was the will of Abba. Whenever it came down to Abba's will versus His own, you always knew where Jesus stood. This characterized His whole life and ministry. Check out these passages from John's Gospel.

"Truly, truly, I say to you, the Son can do nothing of Himself, unless *it is* something He sees the Father doing; for whatever the Father does, these things the Son also does in like manner" (John 5:19 NASB).

"I can do nothing on My own initiative. As I hear, I judge; and My judgment is just, because I do not seek My own will, but the will of Him who sent Me" (John 5:30 NASB).

"I do nothing on My own initiative, but I speak these things as the Father taught Me" (John 8:28 NASB).

"For I did not speak on My own initiative, but the Father Himself who sent Me has given Me a commandment *as to* what to say and what to speak" (John 12:49 NASB).

Isn't it amazing how Jesus could accomplish so much in three years without taking any initiative of His own? He didn't *make* anything happen. Many pastors are A-Type personalities. We're not comfortable waiting around for something to happen. We need to *make* ministry happen. Jesus, however, took time to *listen* to Abba first. The Father informed Him about what to speak, how to speak, when to speak, and with whom to speak. Abba showed Him what to do, how to do it, and when. The Father took the initiative and Jesus followed Him perfectly as an obedient Son.

If you observe Jesus' ministry, He was very active! It is a misconception that ministers who *wait* on the Lord are not busy. The difference is ministers who do more waiting and listening do more God Things! How many of us know that ministry can be done in the flesh?

Jesus was in constant listening mode with Abba. Like David who "inquired of the Lord" (try doing a search on how many times the Bible says David inquired of the Lord), Jesus tuned in to the leading of His heavenly Father and obeyed. What message should He give? He asked Abba. Who is about to be healed? Ask the Father. Which disciples should He select to become the Twelve? He stayed up all night to ask Abba. Jesus listened and then stepped out in obedience. This was the key to the Spirituality of Jesus. And this is the key to our prayer lives as well.

When we pray we do not expand on God's knowledge or understanding of our situation (Matthew 6:8). He knows better than we the precise need of the moment. In fact Scripture says we must rely on the Holy Spirit to intercede on our behalf, for we do not know how or what to pray (Rom. 8:26).

So as we mature in our prayer life it becomes less about informing God and more about listening to God.

How would you characterize your present prayer life? Do you do more "informing" or "listening?" _____

_____

How do we grow in listening prayer? The Altar of Incense is the station where we learn this. During the time of the ancient Tabernacle there was a veil separating the Holy Place from the Holy of Holies. The Altar of Incense would have been located just outside the veil. This suggests that it is the final key to His Presence.

You cannot go beyond the veil unless you first learn the secrets of the Altar of Incense.

Since it is an altar this suggests a sacrifice is made here. Prayer and worship are a pleasing offering to God. "Through Him then, let us continually offer up a sacrifice of praise to God, that is, the fruit of lips that give thanks to His name" (Hebrews 13:15 NASB).

By appearance, like everything inside the Temple, the Altar of Incense was made of Acacia wood covered with gold. The natural (wood) is imbued with the supernatural (gold). According to Exodus 30 it was square-shaped, 18 inches wide, 18 inches long, and 36 inches high.

At dawn and at twilight, Aaron was to offer a specific,

fragrant incense to Lord. He could not offer just any incense. It had to be the one the Lord specified. So incense rose up perpetually before the Lord day and night, generation after generation.

What is the Golden Altar of Incense and what is its significance? _____

_____

What is the significance of burning incense before the Lord?

Remember we said that the Temple is actually a hard-copy of something happening in the spiritual dimension. The Apostle John unlocks the secret of the Altar of Incense in the book of Revelation:

"Another angel, who had a golden censer, came and stood at the altar. He was given much incense to offer, with the prayers of all God's people, on the golden altar in front of the throne. The smoke of the incense, together with the prayers of God's people, went up before God from the angel's hand. Then the angel took the censer, filled it with fire from the altar, and hurled it on the Earth; and there came peals of thunder, rumblings, flashes of lightning and an earthquake" (Revelation 8:3-5 NIV).

The Altar of Incense is our hotline to the Throne of God! Do not miss this point, true believer. In the *actual* Temple of God in the spiritual dimension, the Altar of Incense is the golden altar in the Throne Room of Heaven.

God hears every prayer, every intention of the heart from every life that comes into alignment with His will.

What does the Golden Altar of Incense represent in the heavenly realms? _____

_____

This is why we pray "in Jesus' Name." Praying in Jesus' Name is not some religious tag we put at the end of our prayers. It is not a superstitious phrase we say to "guarantee" that God will answer us. Rather, it conveys a heart willing to submit to the will of Jesus regardless of the outcome.

The Lord assigns an angel to the golden altar. His job is to collect the prayers of God's people, mingle it with Heaven's incense, ignite them with fire from the altar, and hurl it back to the Earth unleashing unspeakable power. The Apostle John's firsthand account of what God does with the prayers of the saints is nothing short of astounding. There is nothing like it anywhere else in Scripture. John reveals the secret power of the Altar of Incense.

What happens at the Altar of Incense in the heavenly dimension? What is the secret of the Golden Altar of Incense? _____

_____

Hear me, friend. As a *Mishkan* Temple of the Holy Presence, there is a Golden Altar of Incense within you. This is not a time for religious, half-hearted prayer. Set aside vain repetitions. You were put here on Earth to do God Things. The Spirit is calling you to the deep places. Prayer is about cultivating a listening heart so you can move in consonance with His will. We do not inform God in prayer, but rather we listen in the Spirit so that we can be informed of what God is doing in our midst.

Spirit-inspired prayer mixed with God's incense form a holy gunpowder that is then ignited by fire from His heavenly Altar, unleashing the power of God on the Earth.

In early 1994 I was walking through a spiritual desert. My reserves were on empty. I was parched and thirsty. Although I had been walking with Jesus since 1975, I knew deep in my heart there was more to God than what I was experiencing.

In *God Things: Encounters with Jesus That Transform Us*, I detail the moment when I was activated in the Holy Spirit and began to pray in a Spiritual language. Living streams began to flow through my soul once again. Praying in the Spirit taught me the secret of the Golden Altar of Incense. I relinquish control over my prayer conversation with God and become more yielded.

Prior to this I was an anti-Charismatic "Baptist-Nazarene," and a Roman Catholic before that. Today I'm clearly Pentecostal. But I still have a Catholic's heart for the poor, a Baptist's love for evangelism, a Nazarene's love of holiness, with a Pentecostal's love for the Holy Spirit. I don't know what I am anymore. I suppose I've become *trans-denominational* in my Spiritual journey since no tradition can adequately describe what I am. So I guess you could say I'm a Roman Bapta-Naza-Costal!

Here's what you need to catch as we end this chapter. I can tell you from God's Word and my personal testimony that there is a deep place of prayer that is *activated* by the Holy Spirit.

I really like the word *activation* in the Spirit better than *baptized* in the Spirit. Let me explain. When we first came to Christ we encountered the Holy Spirit. Like I said in an earlier chapter, we did not meet a man with a beard, robe, and sandals who looked like Jim Caviezel. We met the Spirit of Jesus. So theologically, inasmuch as we use the term "baptism" to mean "initiation," we were baptized in the Spirit at conversion. In the Pentecostal tradition we use the phrase "baptized in the Spirit" to mean a second encounter in the Spirit that releases tongues. But I think the word we're really looking for is *activation*.

Paul says, "Blessed be the God and Father of our Lord Jesus Christ, who has blessed us with every spiritual blessing in the heavenly places in Christ" (Ephesians 1:3 NASB). Did you catch that? We have *every* spiritual blessing. When we come to Christ we *temple* His Spirit within us. This means every blessing, every spiritual resource is available to us by reason of His Presence in us.

I hope this changes your paradigm on spiritual gifts, miracles, prophecies, dreams, visions, and every other spiritual blessing.

Once we know that we *temple* His Spirit, it's more about unwrapping a spiritual gift than asking for one.

It's about *activating* potential we already have rather than trying to be *baptized* into something. This means we really don't "receive" the gift of tongues. The Holy Spirit, who is already present within us since conversion, activates this gift.

The Spirit always does things for a purpose. Just as my conversion sent me on a completely new trajectory in my life, so did the activation of the gift of tongues. Christians do not go around collecting gifts like trophies. When the Spirit moves, it means He is up to something in your life. For me it meant leaving my old ministry and planting a totally different style of ministry with New Hope. It was a radical change for me!

When I pray in my Spiritual language, it is the Holy Spirit praying through me in groanings too deep for words. How do I know that? Because I tried praying in tongues without the Spirit and nothing happened. It happens only through the miraculous activation of the Spirit.

I know it sounds scary to *not* be in control of your prayer life, but what I've learned is that putting *me* in control is a lot scarier! Praying in tongues is a Spiritual gift available to anyone who earnestly desires it. In fact, the Bible urges us to earnestly desire all the gifts (1 Corinthians 14:1), especially prophecy. At first I was seeking the gift of tongues because I wanted to experience this gift. Nothing happened. Then I heard somebody say, "Seek the Giver not the gift." I realized that deep in my heart I really wanted to draw more intimate with Jesus. So I prayed, "Lord, if this gift will transform my prayer life and draw me even closer to You, then I want it!" Not long afterward, the Lord answered my prayer.

So if you sincerely desire a deeper intimacy with God,

then ask the Holy Spirit right now to activate your spiritual language. If you ask your earthly dad for a hamburger, he wouldn't give you a rock would he? So if your imperfect human father knows how to give in the natural, how much more do you think your heavenly Father knows how to give in the supernatural?

If you're not sure how to do this, don't be afraid to ask for help. Go on a personal quest to go deeper in your prayer life.

Is it a requirement to pray in a Spiritual language? Of course not. But since such a powerful prayer resource is available to us, why not pursue it?

A wonderful book that helped me on this matter is *They Speak with Other Tongues* by John Sherrill. I liked it because Sherrill began as a skeptic out to discredit the gift of tongues.

Has your prayer language been activated yet? If not, what is holding you back? If so, have you been using it? _____

_____

The Bible says earnestly desire the Spiritual gifts. As a *Mishkan* Temple of the Spirit you come equipped with a Golden Altar of Incense for supernatural prayer. Let nothing keep you from your full inheritance as a child of God. Like Jesus you too will become a great listener in prayer.

By faith what did the Holy Spirit say to you in this section? How will you obey Him? _____

_____

Part 3

The Holy of Holies

TRANSFORM

The Holy of Holies

TRANSFORM

The greatest interview in the history of the human race was when God talked to Moses. God introduced Himself to Moses as I AM. In Hebrew His Name is Yahweh, or YHWH. The Jews considered His Name so sacred they would not write it on anything they might throw away. They would not even say His Name out loud. They used substitute names for Him like Adonai (Lord), or they would simply refer to Him as Hashem (The Name). This is how greatly they revered the Presence of God. It literally was a reverence bordering on fear.

In the *Mishkan* Temple, Yahweh dwells in the Holy of Holies. It is the deepest place of knowing Jesus. Do you have any idea what it took to bring you here? Jesus Himself became your perfect High Priest. Then He also became the unblemished sacrificial Lamb.

Let's review your amazing odyssey in the Spirit thus far. Your first *connection* with Him was in the Outer Court by salvation at the Bronze Altar and sanctification at the Bronze Basin. Then as you walked into the Temple, you entered the Holy Place. In the context of fellowship with the royal priesthood of believers, the Spirit *equipped* you and things went from bronze to gold. At the Golden Table of Bread, you were equipped to feed your soul with the Word of Life. At the Golden Lamp, you were equipped to share the light of your testimony through serving in ministry. At the Golden Altar of Incense, the Spirit empowered you to pray.

Connect. Equip. What's the final outcome? Transform.

At New Hope Central Oahu we have a saying:

"Transformed lives transform lives."

It means that once our lives have been genuinely changed (and we don't mean perfect) by an encounter with Jesus, we then become agents of that change for the people around us.

Transformation is like fire. When we catch on fire, the fire spreads to the people around us. This is the fire of one who walks in intimacy with the Spirit.

Transformation is like water. The love and compassion of God has been poured into our hearts, and now it is overflowing to everyone around us. The living waters of the Spirit spring forth from our spirit to quench the thirst of everyone we know.

Transformation is like the wind. His power fills our sails with joy, enthusiasm, conviction, resolve, and courage. Just as the wind is unpredictable, so too we allow the Spirit to lead us to the next person He is about to blow away!

Transformation is like a solid rock. Once the Lord truly gets a hold of us there is no shaking us. So in the same way we contend for the Lord to get a hold of people. Once He does, game over! They will never be the same again.

What does "transformed lives transform lives" mean? What happens when we are transformed? _____

_____

As you look up from the Altar of Incense, what do you see? The unveiled Holy of Holies. Directly ahead of you is the Ark of the Covenant covered by the Mercy Seat.

In the Holy Place you encounter the Spirit of God in fellowship with other believers.

Now in the Holy of Holies
you encounter the Spirit
One on one.

If up to this point you saw me as your guide through the Temple of the Spirit, it is here at this moment that I must stay behind. For the Lord calls you into the Holy of Holies to have a One on one encounter with you. No one else can enter with you. It's just you and God now.

The High Priest entered the Holy of Holies alone wearing a very special vestment called an ephod. It had 12 stones representing the 12 Tribes of Israel. Two other stones were called the *Urim* and *Thummim*, meaning *lights* and *perfections* (Exodus 28:30; cf. Numbers 27:21; 1 Samuel 30:7-8; Ezra 2:63; Nehemiah 7:65).

The Urim and Thummim were two stones used to discern the will of God. How they were used exactly is not known. One theory is that if the Urim began to glow it meant God was saying "no." If the Thummim lit up that meant "yes."

Nevertheless, the people turned to the high priest in the Holy of Holies for enlightenment (lights) and perfect knowledge (perfections) of God's will. They looked to him for Spiritual Leadership for the nation of Israel.

Today, you have something far superior than a priestly vestment. The Holy Spirit Himself is your Urim and Thummim. You no longer wear an ephod over your heart because you have the Spirit within your heart. Intimate knowledge of the voice of the Spirit replaces glowing stones.

The Holy of Holies is not just where you receive downloads from the Spirit for your personal life.

The Holy of Holies is also where you receive downloads from the Spirit so you can lead others.

Because you temple the Spirit, there is a Holy of Holies within you. Today you need not depend on a high priest because the Holy Spirit is available to everyone (Joel 2:28-29). When the Holy Spirit leads you, that's called Spiritual Leadership. And He means to empower you to impact the community around you—your people!

The Lord beckons you to enter into His very Presence. The world desperately needs to hear what He tells you in the secret place. Jesus personally tore down the veil so you can experience the deepest recesses of intimacy with God. By the blood of Jesus, you now have an audience with Yahweh.

Why do you think God designed you with a Holy of Holies? _____

_____

Chapter 6
The Ark of the Covenant: Spiritual Leadership

"Inside the Ark were a gold jar containing manna, Aaron's staff that sprouted leaves, and the stone tablets of the covenant" (Hebrews 9:4 NLT).

**Spiritual leadership is about
the Spirit leading leaders
as they lead the people.**

When we say "Spiritual Leadership" we are not talking about spirituality as mysticism. We are talking about the very personal leading of the Holy Spirit—the Spirit of Jesus—in our lives. His leading will be based on the teachings and principles of God's Word, but let's keep it real. You will not find a verse in the Bible that tells you the name of the person you're supposed to marry, which ministry you are to lead, or which nation you are to reach with the Gospel.

What is the definition of Spiritual Leadership? _____

_____

So how do we know these things? These things must be carefully and prayerfully discerned through the Word and Spirit.

Spiritual leadership is not mysticism but it is definitely *mystical.*

Mysticism is an occultic, pagan practice of New Agers to interact with the spirit world.[1] Mystical, however, describes our experience when we deal with a God whose ways are beyond our ways, whose thoughts are higher than our thoughts. Dealing one on one and face to face with God is mystical, but it is not mysticism. That's life here in the Holy of Holies. God will never contradict the Scriptures, but He will reveal His will to leaders in very personal ways. It's called being led by the Spirit or simply, Spiritual Leadership.

You may be thinking, "Mike, are you saying that the Spirit-led life is irrational? Are we supposed to set aside reason and logic and kiss our minds good-bye?" Yes exactly. No! Of course I'm not saying that! The Spirit-led life is both rational and beyond ration. Our minds must be renewed to operate now with the Mind of Christ.

The motto of New Hope Central Oahu is *"Anchored to God's Word and led by His Spirit."* Of course we embrace the full counsel of God's Word. I am simply saying that when we are dealing personally with the Supreme Intelligence in the universe, we may not understand everything, but we still step out in obedience.

Besides, how many of us know that sometimes needing

to understand *everything* first before we obey might be a form of control? We will not be reckless, thoughtless, and undisciplined. But ultimately, we walk by faith not by sight.

Like Abraham who was told to just pack up and go, leaders do not always get to have everything spelled out for us in advance. Besides, to quote one of my favorite theologians, Obiwan Kenobi, "Our eyes can deceive us."

Did it make sense for Noah to build an ark so far from the sea? Was it logical for Moses to stretch out his staff over the Red Sea? Why did Jesus use spit to make mud to heal the blind man? How did Jesus know there would be a coin in the fish's mouth so they could pay their taxes? These things are not contrary to God's Word. Indeed, these testimonies *are* from God's Word!

This is not mysticism, but it is mystical. It is not irrational, but it is beyond mere human rationality.

As I type these words my Church, New Hope Central Oahu, is engaged in an amazing building project. If you know anything about property in Hawaii, then you know that it is scarce and expensive. Our main campus is in a community called Mililani. Since 1999 we have been in rented facilities—school cafeterias and office buildings. That's 16 years as of this writing. And we had two chances to find property in our community—slim and none!

Long story short by the grace of God, we were able to acquire just under 1.5 acres of something called a "storm water quality basin." It took some fancy engineering to come up with the plans that the city would approve, and the project almost died not once but twice.

But praise God for our architect, Charles Kaneshiro, from Group 70, a Christian man with huge faith, who made it happen!

Not only did the Lord reveal this rare piece of property in the exact perfect location, but God also brought a person to our Church who donated the money to purchase the land. So the property is paid in full!

This is what I mean by a God Thing!

The current challenge we face is a $4 million capital campaign for the Church buildings. That is over five times our annual budget. It is a scary thing to follow the Lord in this. But in light of everything else He has done, how could we not step out in faith?

Life at the Ark of the Covenant is about the Spirit leading the leaders who lead God's people.

What is the difference between mysticism and mystical? How does this relate to Spiritual Leadership at the Ark of the Covenant? _____

_____

The Ark of the Covenant was made famous by the Indiana Jones movie, "The "Raiders of the Lost Ark." The ark they were looking for was the Ark of the Covenant. Before the *Mishkan*, the Ark of the Covenant represented the presence of God with His people. There are incredible biblical stories of the supernatural power of God working through the Ark of the Covenant.

So you stand before THAT Ark! You are in the Holy of

Holies.   And the Ark of the Covenant represents the deepest place of intimacy with God.

The Ark is essentially a golden box. The purpose of a box is to contain something.

As a *Mishkan* Temple of the Spirit, there is an "Ark of the Covenant" within you. So what do you contain? Let us open the fabled Ark of the Covenant and find out what is inside of you! Imagine that you are now taking the lid off the Ark of the Covenant and looking inside. (Don't worry, you won't see a hideous ghost that will melt your face!)

The Ark of the Covenant contains three incredibly important items: the Ten Commandments, the Jar of Manna, and the Staff of Aaron.

It is absolutely critical that we understand each one if we are to operate with Spiritual Leadership.

What is the Ark of the Covenant and what is its significance? _____

_____

The Ten Commandments

Let's start with the Ten Commandments. The first mention of the Ten Commandments is in Exodus 20:1-17. As you may recall from the movie with Charlton Heston, these commandments were written by the very finger of God (Exodus 31:18; cf. Deuteronomy 9:10). Translators differ slightly on how to number the commandments. I have opted to go with the original Hebrew listing. Here they are:

The Ten Commandments
1. I AM the Lord your God.
2. You shall have no other gods before Me.[2]
3. Do not take the Name of the Lord your God in vain.[3]
4. Remember the Sabbath Day and keep it holy.
5. Honor your father and mother.
6. You shall not murder.
7. You shall not commit adultery.
8. You shall not steal.
9. You shall not bear false witness against your neighbor.
10. You shall not covet.

Remember that standing in the Holy of Holies before the Ark of the Covenant is about being in the absolute deepest place of intimacy with God. This is where Moses heard the voice of God. Today we call that being led by the Spirit, or Spiritual Leadership. Hearing and obeying go hand in hand. To listen means to obey.

Ever see little children ignore their parents? Mom yells out, "Ok, it's time for bed." But the kids pretend like they didn't hear her and keep on playing. But if mom just whispers, "Let's go to McDonald's," there's a stampede to get in the car. That's called "selective hearing." We can't do that if we want to walk intimately with God. Jesus said that loving God means to listen and obey Him (John 14:15, 23).

When God speaks we hear and obey. The more we obey the better we hear. If we selectively hear only what we want to hear, then hearing God the next time becomes that much more difficult. Sometimes we want God to speak to us, but why should He if we didn't obey Him the last time He spoke? On the other hand, the more we obey the sharper our ability to hear becomes. We become more focused, more attuned to His voice.

Obedience starts with seemingly small, insignificant things like "don't lie" or "don't steal." We think to ourselves, "What's the big deal if I look at this website?" But to God these are huge tests of character and integrity. God knows that if He can trust us with the seemingly little things, then He can trust us with something bigger.

In regard to Spiritual Leadership, what is the relationship between hearing and obeying? _____

_____

The key to hearing God's voice here at the Ark of the Covenant is to cultivate a heart of obedience. Here are three key observations to cooperate with the Spirit to cultivate a heart of obedience.

First, notice that the first four commandments are "vertical." That is, they have to do with honoring God. The last six are "horizontal." They have to do with loving people. This is in keeping with God's greatest commandment, "Love God with all your heart, soul, mind, and strength, and your neighbor as yourself." Loving and obeying God has to do with a commitment to both God and people. But it goes beyond that.

Genesis tells us "In the beginning God created the heavens and the earth" (Genesis 1:1). As *Mishkan* Temples of His Spirit we are a unique hybrid of Heaven and Earth, the vertical and the horizontal. God in Heaven (vertical) formed us from the Earth (horizontal) then breathed His Spirit (vertical) into us (horizontal). We are earthen, horizontal vessels infused with vertical, heavenly power.

Then God put us in charge of the Earth, to take dominion over it, to take care of it. This is why Jesus taught us to pray, "Thy Kingdom come, Thy will be done on Earth as it is in Heaven." To cultivate a heart of obedience means to be responsible for loving both God in Heaven and people on Earth. Through us Heaven touches Earth with transformational power.

The point is that we cannot truly love others unless we are in loving relationship with God. Only through our connection with God can we rightly connect with others.

Men, would you want to be led by a pastor who isn't led by the Lord? Wives, would you want to be led by a husband who isn't led by the Spirit? Children, would you want to be led by parents who aren't submitted to God's leadership?

Why did God make the first four commandments about obeying Him and the final six about loving others? ____

Second, you should know that God did not give the Ten Commandments to us so we could earn our salvation. He gave them to a people He already saved so they would learn how to co-exist with a holy God. He didn't give them to the Hebrews while they were in bondage to Egypt and say, "If you can obey these commandments, then I will deliver you." Instead, He saved His people with supernatural signs and miraculous wonders by *grace*—there's that word again describing salvation in the Old Testament. Then after they were freed from slavery and camped at the foot of Mount Sinai, God gave them the Ten Commandments.

The Hebrews were saved by grace *first* and then given the Ten Commandments *second*.

Once God freed them from slavery, then He could teach them how to live free. So the purpose of the Ten Commandments is not legalism but intimacy with God. He wants to teach us how to be holy as He is holy so we can experience the full blessing of intimate friendship with Him.

Why is it important to know that God saved the Hebrews first before giving them the Ten Commandments?

_____

_____

Third, only through the Holy Spirit's empowering presence can we live in obedience. "I'll put my Spirit in you and make it possible for you to do what I tell you and live by my commands" (Ezekiel 36:27 MSG). It is not possible to fulfill the Ten Commandments unless we temple the Spirit. God's ultimate goal for us is not holiness for holiness sake but intimacy with Him.

I remember the first time I heard about the Ten Commandments I thought the reason God gave them to us was to make us morally good. But it is impossible to obey the commandments in our own strength. And God knows that! The purpose of the Ten Commandments is not just morality but intimacy with God. And in order to be intimate we must be holy and obedient.

However, we are in a Catch 22. We cannot be intimate with God unless we are holy and obedient, and we cannot be holy and obedient apart from intimacy with God! So Ezekiel prophesied a time when the Lord would give us His Spirit to empower us to obey. That time is now!

We are living in the Age of the Spirit when God not only gives us His moral laws, but empowers us with His Presence to fulfill them.

Attempting to fulfill His laws without His Presence leads to moralism and self-righteousness. We will either give up in failure and/or just accept our hypocrisy.

On the other hand, learning a heart of obedience *in the Spirit* leads to humility, grace, truth, and loving intimacy with God.

Are you starting to get the picture here? God is all about intimacy with us. In order to be intimate with a holy God we will need to be holy.

To parallel what Ezekiel says check this out:

"I will imprint My laws upon their minds, even upon their innermost thoughts and understanding, and engrave them upon their hearts; and I will be their God, and they shall be My people" (Hebrews 8:10 cf. 10:16 AMP).

As *Mishkan* Temples, God not only gives us a new heart to obey Him, He also imprints His law onto our hearts. This means that a person who temples the Spirit will have a renewed mind to know good and evil, right and wrong in every situation.

What do Ezekiel and Hebrews say is the answer to being holy and intimate? _____

_____

We will not experience His shalom peace unless we live in obedience to God's commands. The Spirit will tell us when we have transgressed the Law. But as we choose to live in holy intimacy with Him, we grow in our love and confidence in God. We not only know in our minds that He loves us, we feel His love in our hearts.

As we become more assured of His love, we become bolder! And this is awesome because the second item in the Ark of the Covenant reveals how critical it is to God that we cultivate a heart of faith.

The Jar of Manna

Each time we obey God we get to see Him at work in our lives. When we see God at work we grow in faith and confidence.

I remember when Mona and I first sensed that God was leading us out of youth ministry into something new. We weren't sure what our new ministry would be yet, but we discerned that He was calling us to spend a season in seminary. Seminary requires money.

One night a good friend and I were driving in the car and he asked me, "So Mike, how do you plan to pay for seminary?" Just as I was about to respond a $20 bill blew across the windshield! Instead of responding to him I yelled out, "Hey! That was money!" I pulled over the side of the road, walked back a few yards, and found the $20 bill in the grass.

I wasn't sure how I was going to pay for seminary, but the Lord showed me that night, "This is how you will pay for seminary." Sure enough God was faithful. In 1998 I graduated from Regent College in Vancouver, BC with a Master's degree in Christian Studies.

When God delivered His people from bondage in Egypt, there was no question that was God Thing. You don't topple the greatest military power in the region through ten plagues unless God is with you. It was God who split the Red Sea. God led them with a cloud by day and a pillar of fire by night.

So in the same way, today the Cross is the power of God for the salvation of all mankind. Jesus leads us out of slavery to sin to freedom in the Spirit.

Here's the thing. When the Hebrews left Egypt they left in a big hurry. The night before was Passover. The next day they left Egypt as quickly as possible (before Pharaoh could change his mind again!). So they walked into their new lives with just the clothes on their backs and light provisions. They simply followed Moses into the wilderness. Imagine that!

They had no idea where they were going, no place to sleep, and whatever food and water they were carrying was going to run out very quickly. They had their freedom, but now they had to completely trust Moses, their Spiritual leader, and God for their very survival. It's the craziest thing a million people have ever done together!

This is why there is a Jar of Manna in the Ark of the Covenant. Being a slave was a horrible life, but at least they could count on their Egyptian masters to feed them and give them a place to sleep. Egyptians did that for their horses, pets, and slaves. Now the Hebrews were free, but this meant they had to take care of themselves. They had to depend on God to take care of them, not the Egyptians.

The day finally came when all their food was gone. Their stomachs rumbled so the people grumbled. And they turned on Moses. The very man who Spiritually led them to freedom was now going to be held responsible for starving them to death in the desert. In Exodus 16 the Bible records that the people said things like, "In Egypt we had all we could eat. Better to die a slave with a full a stomach than starve to death as a free person." Hunger does that to a person.

But God did not set His people free only to see them perish in the wilderness. The Lord told Moses to tell the people, "Behold, I will rain bread from the heavens for you" (Exodus 16:4 AMP). The next day they looked on the ground and saw a flaky substance and said, "What is it?" And they've been calling it that ever since. In Hebrew "manna" means "what is it?" We might say, "That's what-cha-ma-call-it."

Miraculously God also provided quail and water despite all their grumblings. The point is "where God guides He provides."[4] It was a God Thing they were saved. They were in the center of God's will as He was forming them into a holy nation, a people for His own possession. He wasn't going to save them only to let them die in the wilderness. They just needed to cultivate a heart of faith.

Being led by the Holy Spirit requires faith. Our faith grows every time we experience God's faithfulness. And the only way we will experience God's faithfulness is to step out in faith. As the people stepped out of slavery into freedom, so in the same way we step out of our past lives of sin into freedom in Christ. We may not be able to count on our old friends or even our family. We need to have faith in God now, the author and perfecter of our faith.

There is a Jar of "What-Is-It?" within every person who temples the Spirit.

As we follow Christ on our great adventure, leaders will be faced with many situations where we scratch our heads and ask, "What is it?" "What's going on?" "Why did that just happen?"

God doesn't always tells us how things are supposed to work out. He just tells us to trust Him. That way leaders learn firsthand that He is trustworthy!

When you think about it, the reason we feel fear and anxiety is because we live in a time-space continuum. This means events unfold. We don't always know how things will turn out. This can cause fear, anxiety, and nervousness.

However, since God exists in eternity, He doesn't have that problem. He sees the start and the finish simultaneously. He knows how the movie ends. So He is never worried, never anxious, never afraid.

He knows everything works out for good to those who love Him. There will always be temporary setbacks. But when we walk by faith hand in hand with God, we too can set aside all worry, anxiety, and fear. Why? Because we know God's got this.

The Jar of Manna is a reminder from eternity that God will be faithful in the temporary.

In what situation is God calling you right now to walk by faith and not by sight? _____

_____

The Ark of the Covenant teaches leaders that a heart of obedience and faith increases a leader's authority levels in life and ministry. Next let's talk about authority.

The Staff of Aaron

The third item inside the Ark of the Covenant, the Staff of Aaron, has to do with divinely given authority. Coming under the authority of God does not constrain us, it sets us free. Coming under the authority of God is the key to greater authority in Spiritual Leadership. Sounds good so far. But here's the part we have trouble with: If we say we come under God's authority, this means we come under the authority of those He placed as Spiritual leaders over us!

This is called *submission*.

There are no perfect pastors. King Saul was a terrible leader, yet David submitted to him. Saul's rage was out of control, and he even tried to murder David. Once David had an opportunity to assassinate Saul. David's men begged him to do it. But David decided, "I will not lift a hand against the Lord's anointed."[5]

David understood the teaching of the Staff of Aaron. He

knew that although Saul was a horrible leader, it was not his place to supplant him. David knew that God appointed Saul as king, and coming against Saul meant coming against God. David wouldn't go there.

There are no perfect pastors. Sometimes it's not easy to obey what a Spiritual leader is asking. Ultimately, however, we get to trust that God knew what He was doing when He appointed this pastor.

A long time ago in a galaxy far far away, I felt it was time for me to move on from the ministry I had been a part of for 16 years. When I shared this with my Spiritual leader, he gave me permission to leave but asked me to stay two more years. "Two more years?" I thought to myself. I didn't want to stay two more days much less two more years! But I believed in the principle of submission to God's leaders. So I stayed two more years.

A year into my extended term, the Lord initiated an amazing move of the Spirit in Hawaii called New Hope. Under the leadership of Pastor Wayne Cordeiro, New Hope Oahu grew to 3,000 people in one year! I never saw anything like this before. It was a God Thing. Since I was interested in planting church I joined New Hope to learn all I could. I got to spend a full year being mentored by Pastor Wayne before heading off to seminary. After I returned I planted New Hope Mililani, the first church plant out of New Hope Oahu.

Do you see how submission to authority yielded an immeasurable blessing to me, my family, and my community? If I had told my previous Spiritual leader, "Two years? No way! I'm on the next plane out of here," I would have missed my opportunity to see the Holy Spirit birth New Hope. I wouldn't have become friends with Pastor Wayne who remains a valuable mentor in my life. I would not have been introduced to the very ministry I would join after returning from seminary.

There are no perfect pastors. But as we submit to authority, we learn that even imperfect pastors cannot keep us from God's best!

Coming under submission to Spiritual authority is key to greater Spiritual authority in your life.

I know that sounds paradoxical. It seems like the opposite would be true. If you're fighting in Mixed Martial Arts you want to avoid a submission hold. The least popular verse in the bible is "wives be submitted to your husbands." Nobody likes submission, especially in America. This is a country that overthrew a king and created a government run by "we the people." So submission is not a popular word in our society. We don't like people telling us what to do.

Consider this, however: If you are a student and you do everything your teacher tells you, what grade will you likely get in class? Probably an "A." Why? Because you came under the authority of your teacher. What if your teacher gives you one assignment but you decide to do your own thing? Now what grade would you get? Why? You didn't come under authority. You don't get to graduate to the next grade.

If you are in the military and you do what your commanding officer says, you'll do great. You might even be promoted. Why? You came under the authority of your superior officer. But if you disobey orders, then what happens? You'll get written up, maybe face a court-martial. You don't get promoted.

In Church the same axiom holds true. Those who do their own thing end up making the same mistakes over and over. They may go to Church for 30 years, but all they did was repeat year one 30 times. Those who submit to Spiritual authority increase in Spiritual authority.

In the beginning God authorized man to take dominion over the Earth, that means to rule the world. It is our destiny to do so—to take dominion over the fish of the sea and the birds of the air. The whole Earth was supposed to come under the authority of Adam. But what happened? Adam gave his authority to the Serpent.

Now follow this closely: God gave Adam the authority to rule the Earth, but when he disobeyed God he lost that authority. So when Adam no longer submitted himself to the authority of God, Adam lost authority over the Earth. So who became ruler of the Earth? You guessed it. This is why the devil is called the "ruler of this world" (John 12:31; 14:30) or the "god of this world" (2 Corinthians 4:4).

Once mankind came under the authority of the devil, we put the Earth under the devil's authority.

Why is the world broken and in such despair? We have no one to blame but ourselves.

So how do we get our rightful authority back? This is yet another reason the finished work of Jesus on the Cross is His magnum opus! The words of Jesus: "Now judgment is upon this world; now the ruler of this world will be cast out" (John 12:31 NASB). By paying the full penalty for Adam's sin on the cross, Jesus (the second Adam) broke the authority of the devil over mankind and made a way for us to come back under the authority of the Father! What happens when we come back under God's authority? Exactly! We can now retake dominion over the Earth.

This is why the proper exercise of submission is the key to greater authority. Remember that the reason that Jesus could do all the amazing things He did was because He lived perfectly under the authority of the Father. When we get this, then we live with greater authority!

In terms of Spiritual Leadership what does "submission" mean? _____

_____

There's a difference between participating in a ministry and leading one, between attending church and pastoring one. Spiritual Leadership is about God calling us to lead something, whether it is your family, work, or ministry. This means you are in charge. You have authority. What has God put you in charge of?

Have you ever been to a church where the pastor did *not* come under the authority of the Spirit? It is not a happy place. It is either feckless and ineffective or manic and depressive! You either sit there desperately trying to stay awake or you burn out trying to do the countless man-driven things the pastor says.

By contrast have you ever been to a Church where the

pastor tried to follow the leadership of the Holy Spirit? It is scary and exciting (in a good way)! You are constantly in awe of God in worship and in what He is doing in your midst. The teaching speaks to your heart and transforms your life. People come to Christ as they encounter Jesus in answered prayer, dreams, visions, and miracles. The Spirit empowers you to love and serve Jesus beyond your wildest dreams or expectations.

But Church is not the only setting where we need leaders who are filled and led by the Holy Spirit. Dads need to be Spiritual leaders. Moms need to be. Youth can be Spiritual leaders to their classmates. We need Spiritual leaders from all walks of life—business, politics, education, entertainment, medicine, etc. Every facet of society needs Spiritual leaders!

This is why God places a Staff of Aaron in your heart.

The world needs Spiritual leaders who operate with Spiritual authority.

How does coming under submission to authority increase your Spiritual authority? _____

_____

There is an Ark of the Covenant within each leader who temples the Spirit. Here at this amazing station, the Lord teaches leaders three huge lessons on how to be a leader who is led by the Spirit. He empowers us to have a heart of obedience, a heart of faith, and a heart of authority.

Now we are ready for the seventh and final station of

the Temple.

By faith what did the Holy Spirit say to you in this
section? How will you obey Him? _____

_____

_____

1. See 1 Samuel 28 where King Saul is frustrated that
the Lord will not answer him and so he seeks out a
medium or spiritist—sometimes referred to as the Witch
of Endor—in order to conjure up Samuel from the afterlife.   This is an example of "mysticism" which is not to
be confused with "mystical."
2. Literally in Hebrew, you shall have no other gods
before My face.
3. Literally in Hebrew, do not take the Name of the Lord
your God in a reckless or careless way.
4. I first heard this phrase from Pastor Rick Warren of
Saddleback Church.
5. See 1 Samuel 24.

Chapter 7
The Mercy Seat:
Great Commission

"There I will meet with you and, from above the Mercy Seat, from between the two cherubim that are upon the ark of the Testimony, I will speak intimately with you of all which I will give you in commandment to the Israelites" (Exodus 25:22 AMP).

**To be an effective Spiritual leader
we not only need to know how to be
led by the Holy Spirit,
we need to know God's end game.**

When we go on a journey, we want to know the final destination. Imagine a football game with no end zone: "He's to the 20! The 10! The 5! He's...leaving the stadium?!" Or a family vacation with no destination planned. "Where are we flying to, daddy?" "Oh, no where in particular, we're just flying."

Effective businesses have clear goals and targets. Any effective organization knows what they're trying to produce. But what about Churches? What is the final "product" of Church?

What is God's end game?

As people come to Church, we must ask the question, "What does *God* want them to ultimately *be* and *do*?" A fully mature disciple of Jesus is about both *being* and *doing.*

How does a fully mature disciple BE?
He walks intimately with God
in loving relationship.

What does a fully mature disciple DO?
He helps others walk intimately with God
in loving relationship.

I contend that the Lord has made our final destination clear in the *Mishkan* Temple template that He gave us. Just to remind ourselves, the Temple template originates from God not man.

This vision is not birthed out of "many years of doing church." It does not originate from the experiences of a panel of pastoral experts. It comes from the heart of God.

Church leaders do not need to come up with an end game. We need to understand it, then implement it.

On our odyssey through the Temple, we have reached our final destination according to God's roadmap. It is the Mercy Seat which covers the Ark of the Covenant. As seen above in Exodus 25:22, this is where God spoke intimately with Moses about God's will for Israel.

The Mercy Seat is about God leading you so you can lead the people He told you to lead.

You may be the lead pastor of a Church, or you may be a parent. You may be a businessman, an educator, a political leader, or some other professional. Whatever God has called you to lead will require you to be a person who knows how to be led by His Spirit.

Through Jesus God has given us His end game in no uncertain terms. God's end game of *being* and *doing* can be summed up in the Great Commission—the Lord's final command to make disciples who make disciples who make disciples who make disciples, etc. And what we will see is that this was foreshadowed in an astounding way in what the high priest was doing at the Mercy Seat. What did the high priest do at the Mercy Seat? Patience, my friend. We will come to that.

What is God's end game for Church? _____

_____

When we first start out on our journey of faith we hear people say, "Come!" "Come to Christ." "Come to Church." "Come to small group." "Come to bible study." But at the end of our journey we are told, "Go!" "Go lead people to Christ." "Go make disciples." "Go to the remotest parts of the Earth." First we come, then we go.

Between come and go is *become*. We *come* to Christ. His Spirit transforms us to *become* lightning in a bottle. Then we *go* to the world with His presence and power to help others come, become, and go.

When I was little and did something naughty my mom used to say, "Mike, you are becoming very unbecoming!" We don't want to un-become like me, we want to become!

At the end of our journey through the *Mishkan* Temple—here at the Mercy Seat—we are sent to the world to bring people to the Outer Court so they can begin their odyssey to temple the Spirit. We *come* to the Bronze Altar; we *go* from the Mercy Seat.

Since we temple the Holy Spirit, there is a Mercy Seat within us. This is where the Spirit of God speaks to leaders. Like Moses heard the voice of God at the Mercy Seat, so too leaders hear the voice of the Holy Spirit at the Mercy Seat within our hearts.

What does He say to us? First, He pours out His love for us through the Holy Spirit (being). "The love of God has been poured out within our hearts through the Holy Spirit who was given to us" (Romans 5:5 NASB).

Simultaneously, the Holy Spirit empowers us to tell the world of His love (doing). "But you will receive power when the Holy Spirit has come upon you; and you shall be My witnesses both in Jerusalem, and in all Judea and Samaria, and even to the remotest part of the Earth" (Acts 1:8 NASB).

This is at the core of the Father heart of God. He downloads His love into us, then we upload love for others.

It's not, "OMG, do I have to share the Gospel with other people? That's so scary!" It's more like, "Oh God, nothing will stop me from telling the whole world about Your amazing love!" When you are downloading love from

God and uploading love for others, that's a clear sign you are hearing the voice of God.

Jot down the Holy Spirit's words of love to you. How does this affect your love for others? _____

_____

This is our experience these days at the Mercy Seat. God continues to speak very intimately with us today. Jesus said, "I am with you always, even to the end of the age" (Matthew 28:20 NASB). This is a co-mission with Jesus. He will be right there with us every step of the way. He is after all the Lord of the harvest. Are you searching for Jesus? You'll find Him in the harvest.

Being and doing fuse together in this amazing thing called the Great Commission.

We know that everything in the *Mishkan* Temple parallels something in the heavenly dimension. The seven stations are a hardcopy of things in the Spirit. What exactly is the Mercy Seat, and what is its parallel in the heavenly Kingdom?

The Mercy Seat, or *Kapporet* (Hebrew) comes from a root word that means "cover." Its Greek counterpart, *Hilarios* means propitiation. Like everything else in the Holy of Holies it is covered with gold.

It was Martin Luther who first coined the phrase "Mercy Seat," but it is not an actual seat to sit on. It's more like a lid for the Ark of the Covenant. It had two angels or cherubim on top with their wings outstretched toward one the center.

So this is the place of covering under angelic protection and propitiation for sin for the sake of access and intimacy with God.

What is the Mercy Seat and how is it related to God's end game? _____

_____

But whose sin? Who needs atonement with God? Our sin was dealt with at the Bronze Altar, remember? There is no way to even begin our relationship with God apart from salvation through Jesus and the Cross. So who is in need of atonement now?

Let's rewind the tape on biblical history to see the significance of the Mercy Seat and the answer to this question.

According to Leviticus 16, once a year on Yom Kippur (the Day of Atonement) the Jewish high priest—and *only* the high priest—is permitted to pass beyond the veil and enter the Holy of Holies. During the time of Leviticus this was Aaron, the brother of Moses.

"The Lord said to Moses, tell Aaron your brother he must not come at all times into the Holy of Holies within the veil before the Mercy Seat upon the Ark, lest he die; for I will appear in the cloud on the Mercy Seat" (Leviticus 16:2 AMP).

So the Mercy Seat is the location of the glory of God, or Shekhinah (Hebrew). We say Manifest Presence because God, who is typically invisible, now becomes detectable or manifest to us in this moment. God appears above the Mercy Seat in the cloud. In the Outer Court we experience His Manifest Presence in Salvation and Sanctification. In the Holy Place we experience His Manifest Presence in fellowship with others centered in the Scriptures, Testimony, and Prayer.

In the Holy of Holies—before the Mercy Seat— we experience the very Person of God in a One on one encounter, Spirit to spirit.

The Spirit of Jesus and our spirit unite. This is an encounter with the Holy Spirit in our heart, soul, mind, and body. It is an AWESOME place! YOU are AWESOME! Because you are the *Mishkan* Temple of the Holy Spirit, God is amazing in you. To relate to God in this manner is the reason you were created.

At the Mercy Seat describe the relationship you have with God. _____

_____

The Presence of God is a heavy matter. Moses told Aaron not to approach the Mercy Seat anytime or anyway he wanted, "lest he die." We cannot approach the Presence of God on our terms. To do so is a capital offense. We come on God's terms or perish in the attempt. Legend has it that a rope was tied to the high priest's ankle or waist so he could be hauled out of the Holy of Holies in case he dropped dead. This has been oft repeated but I could not find a reference to this in either the Bible or Jewish tradition. But true or not, point taken!

So what does God require before entering His Presence? Aaron was told to be sure to sacrifice a bull on behalf of his own sin and a ram for a burnt offering. So at the Bronze Altar, he had to be sure of his own rightness before God. As for us we gain access to Him by the blood of Jesus. Jesus didn't die just to get us to Heaven. He died in order to bring us here into the Father's very Presence.

But then Aaron was to take two choice goats. Let's switch gears now and focus on these two goats. Back outside in the Outer Court, lots were cast before God. One goat was set free into the wilderness of Azazel. Aaron placed his hands on this goat, confessed all the sins of the nation of Israel upon it, and then set it free.

The Azazel goat was allowed to escape even though it bore all the sins of the nation. This is where we get the term "scapegoat." Are you starting to get the picture here? A guilty nation gets set free.

What about the other goat? It was cast to Yahweh. Its life was sacrificed for sin—the innocent for the guilty. Again God teaches the need for a substitutionary death because of sin. The life blood of an innocent is shed on behalf of a guilty nation.

Now Aaron (and every high priest after him) was asked to do an unusual thing. He took a portion of the blood of Yahweh's goat (plus some blood from his own offering to include himself) and took it beyond the veil and stood before the Mercy Seat.

He now stands before the Mercy Seat in the deepest place of intimacy with almighty God. What is he doing in there? Using his fingers Aaron proceeds to sprinkle the Mercy Seat with the blood. What is this all about?

The central question is *whose* sin is being atoned for at the Mercy Seat. Aaron is no longer just contending for his own sin. The sacrifices brought to the Bronze Altar were for individual sin. However, here at the Mercy Seat, on Yom Kippur—the one occasion he was permitted to go beyond the veil—Aaron intercedes for the whole nation.

It is a powerful ritual that exposes the heart of God for the world. What an amazing revelation of what resides in the deepest recesses of the mind of God! In this rare glimpse, we see His heart for every nation—all peoples —to be saved and come to know Him intimately. God opens His heart to us and unveils His most intimate desire—for His children to come home.

Before the Mercy Seat the high priest atones for the sins of the nation.

What does the high priest do before the Mercy Seat? What does this say about God? _____

_____

Remember that everything that takes place in the *Mishkan* Temple is a "hardcopy" of something happening in the spiritual dimension. The blood of bulls, goats, and rams could never take away individual sin, much less the sin of nations. So we need to see it with spiritual eyes. What is going on, Lord? Show us more!

Fast forward to Jesus. Jesus is standing before Pontius Pilate. Who else is brought before Pilate? Barabbas. Bar-abbas. His name means "son of Abba." One of these will be set free, the other crucified. "This will not be on my head," Pilate reasons. He knows Jesus is innocent, but he is a weak leader. He allows the mob to rule. He casts lots to escape responsibility. The lot falls to Jesus. Barabbas, the convicted criminal, the sinner, is set free. He is Azazel—the scapegoat. Jesus is the Son of Yahweh. The blood of an Innocent is shed for the sins of the world.

Jesus becomes the sacrifice to Yahweh on behalf of the sins of the nations.

At the Mercy Seat what did the goat sacrifices foreshadow? _____

_____

What does the Mercy Seat represent in the heavenly Kingdom? The book of Revelation shows us that the Mercy Seat is actually a hardcopy of the Throne of God (Revelation 4; cf. 11:19). Martin Luther was not far from the truth after all. In Heaven the Mercy Seat actually *is* a seat—the seat of all power and authority in the universe. According to Hebrews, Jesus is the true High Priest.

Jesus, the true High Priest, stood before the actual Mercy Seat in the Kingdom of Heaven, which is the Throne of God, and sprinkled it with His own blood so that every tribe and nation could receive mercy from God.

It is entirely befitting that a blood-sprinkled Throne represents the gracious Presence of God. Listen to Abba say to the nations of the world, "Enter! My mercy and grace cover you; your sin is forgiven through the perfect sacrifice of My Son, Jesus." This is the declaration from the true Throne in the heavenly dimension, the true Mercy Seat in Heaven. He bids us to enter. He has removed the ancient veil that separated us from Him since the Fall.

What does Jesus, the true High Priest, do before the Mercy Seat in Heaven? _____

_____

There is a Mercy Seat within each disciple of Jesus, a blood-sprinkled Throne. His Throne means authority—all the authority of Heaven and Earth. Jesus did not die and rise again just so you could go to Heaven. He died so Heaven's authority could be within you! For what purpose? To make disciples of all nations. To cover the sins of the nations by His blood.

"After being made alive, He (Jesus) went and made proclamation to the imprisoned spirits—to those who were disobedient long ago when God waited patiently in the days of Noah while the ark was being built. In it only a few people, eight in all, were saved through water, and this water symbolizes baptism that now saves you also—not the removal of dirt from the body but the pledge of a clear conscience toward God. It saves you by the resurrection of Jesus Christ, who has gone into Heaven and is at God's right hand—with angels, authorities and powers in submission to Him" (1 Peter 3:19-22 NIV).

At the Cross Jesus won a sweeping victory for all mankind that positioned Him "at God's right hand with angels, authorities and powers in submission to Him." His finished work on the cross is the key! This is precisely why after His Resurrection and before His Ascension, Jesus said, "All authority in Heaven and on Earth has been given to Me" (Matthew 28:18 NIV).

In the spiritual dimension He now speaks from His Throne of ultimate authority over the universe—the Mercy Seat. This is why the Gospel is the power of God for salvation.

So when Jesus encounters the disciples after His resurrection, He speaks as One who wields all the authority in the universe. And while wielding ultimate, universal authority, what exactly does He say? This is exciting and very revealing!

"All authority in Heaven and on Earth has been given to me. Therefore go and make disciples of all nations, baptizing them in the name of the Father and of the Son and of the Holy Spirit, and teaching them to obey everything I have commanded you. And surely I am with you always, to the very end of the age" (Mt. 28:18-20 NIV).

This is an astounding download directly from the Mercy Seat in the Throne room of God. Jesus returns from the dead to personally convey this message to His disciples. Jesus gives us a rare perspective on life from One who was dead, went to Heaven, and returned back to life. This comes from the Mercy Seat, the very Presence of God.

What is on God's heart? What is so precious and sacred to God that He would allow only His chosen High Priest, His only begotten Son, to contend for on this day of all days? The nations. The people of the Earth. God's heart has not changed since the days of Moses. In the ancient *Mishkan* God contended for His children to come home. In the modern *Mishkan*, He contends for that still.

Now do you see the connection between the Mercy Seat and the Great Commission? From the Throne of the Universe, the King of kings sends us forth to make disciples of all nations, to teach them to obey Him. Now because of the perfect sacrifice of Yahweh, the precious blood of Jesus can cover the whole Earth. His Spirit empowers us to do this. His Presence is with us to the very end of time, and to the remotest parts of the Earth.

How is the Mercy Seat connected with the Great Commission of Jesus? _____

_____

The Great Commission was never something we were supposed to do *for* God. The Great Commission is something we do *with* God.

Jesus is the Alpha and the Omega, the Aleph and the Tav, the first and the last. He is the Author and the Finisher of our faith. He is the keeper of our destiny. When He created us He also wrote the purpose for our lives at the same time.

Before He formed us in our mother's womb He knew us. How can He know someone who does not yet exist? We were a thought in the mind of God. This means He thought through our entire lives beforehand. God never does anything without a strong purpose. This means He first had a purpose in mind and then second created a person to fulfill that purpose.

God has a divine purpose for every person.

Now watch this. God's heart longed to reach His lost

children in India, so He created William Carey. Then God's heart yearned for His kids in China, so He created Hudson Taylor. His heart longed for the people of Hawaii so He created Henry 'Ōpūkaha'ia who inspired Hiram Bingham to travel thousands of miles from Boston to plant the very first Christian Church in the islands.

This has continued generation after generation so that today one-third of mankind worships at the feet of Jesus. God's heart continues to long for every people group—every nation—in the world today. So He continues to create people designed to reach them.

Who did God design you to reach for Jesus? _____

_____

Have you ever wished you could talk to someone who had come back from the dead? Besides the resurrection of Jesus, the Bible records several other resurrections—Jairus' daughter, the son of the widow of Nain, the boy Elijah raised up, and Lazarus.

But we get so few details of the afterlife from those guys. It's frustrating that nobody thought of interviewing these people to ask them what they experienced!

With Jesus, however, the Bible records numerous post-resurrection conversations. And perhaps this is fitting since He would have the greatest authority to speak on the afterlife.

With all the authority of the Throne of Heaven, Jesus tells us to go make disciples who make disciples who make disciples who...

If I can paraphrase, Jesus comes back from His heavenly Mercy Seat—His Throne—to say:

"Take it from Someone who was dead and came back to life, the only thing that's going to matter for all eternity is being My disciple."

People spend more time thinking about how they will live their last ten years on Earth than they do their first 10 million years in eternity.

What is the most important thing we can *be* and *do* in life from the perspective of Jesus who returned from the afterlife? _____

_____

Through the Temple template, the Lord gives us a profound picture of how we can experience His Manifest Presence. I propose that He is offering us a Divine design on how to structure a local Church.

When someone comes to your Church, how would you like them to turn out? What would a fully mature disciple of Christ look like in your Church culture?

What is God's end game?

When the Bible says "Temple of the Spirit," it means we are a people who host the Presence of God. This is equally about both *being* and *doing*. We are Abba's children in loving, intimate relationship with our Father. Simultaneously, we are effective in evangelism and discipleship. To the end of the age, we experience God's empowering Presence as we work in His harvest. We manifest both the character and mission of Jesus through our lives on a daily basis.

In summary how does the Mercy Seat within you empower you to lead what God called you to lead? _____

_____

By faith what did the Holy Spirit say to you in this section? How will you obey Him? _____

_____

Epilogue

Aftermath

The darkest day in the history of Israel is called the Ninth of Av. It was August 14, 586 BC when King Nebuchadnezzar of Babylon sent Nebuzaradan, the captain of his guard, to destroy Jerusalem (2 Kings 25:8-11; cf. 2 Chronicles 36:17-21). Solomon's Temple, the center of life for all Israel, was destroyed. After the destruction of the Temple, the people of Israel were exiled for 70 years in accordance with prophecy (Jeremiah 25:12; 29:10).

What is the darkest day in Israel's history? _____

_____

Then, beyond all hope, they miraculously returned from exile and rebuilt the Temple. This rebuilding was the context for the book of Haggai. The Prophet Haggai exhorted the leaders:

"But now the Lord says: Be strong, Zerubbabel. Be strong, Jeshua son of Jehozadak, the high priest. Be strong, all you people still left in the land. And now get to work, for I am with you, says the Lord of Heaven's Armies. My Spirit remains among you, just as I promised when you came out of Egypt. So do not be afraid (Haggai 2:4-5 NLT).

Haggai's words are just as relevant and urgent to us Temple builders today. In short the Lord says to us: "Be strong, be strong, be strong! And get to work. Do not be afraid. The Spirit of the Living God dwells within you."

Haggai the prophet went on to say, "For this is what the

Lord of Heaven's Armies says: In just a little while I will again shake the heavens and the Earth, the oceans and the dry land. I will shake all the nations and the treasures of all the nations will be brought to this Temple. I will fill this place with glory, says the Lord of Heaven's Armies. The silver is mine, and the gold is mine, says the Lord of Heaven's Armies. *The future glory of this Temple will be greater than its past glory* (italics mine), says the Lord of Heaven's Armies. And in this place I will bring peace. I, the Lord of Heaven's Armies, have spoken!" (Haggai 2:6-9 NLT).

Did you catch the last part? Haggai prophesies, "The future glory of this Temple will be greater than its past glory."

What did Haggai prophesy about the next Temple? ____

_____

When they returned from exile, the people of Israel did indeed rebuild the Temple. However, the glory of this Temple was nowhere near the glory of Solomon's Temple. In fact, it fell so short of expectations that the Jews renovated the Temple under King Herod. This became known as Herod's Temple just before the time of Christ.

Even after renovation, however, it could not honestly be assessed that Herod's Temple surpassed the glory of the original Solomon's Temple. So when Haggai prophesied, "The future glory will be greater than its past glory," to which Temple did he refer?

In Matthew 24 Jesus, who, in addition to being the Messiah, was the most accurate prophet who ever lived, gazed upon Herod's Temple in Jerusalem and said: "Do you see all these things?" he asked. "Truly I tell you, not one stone here will be left on another; every one will be thrown down" (Matthew 24:2 NIV). Jesus prophesied the total destruction of Herod's Temple in Jerusalem.

Sure enough in 70 AD the Romans destroyed Herod's Temple. Do you know the date it was destroyed? The Ninth of Av. Both Temples were destroyed on the same date over six centuries apart! The exact same date! Clearly God is highlighting this moment with big bold letters. What is God trying to tell us?

The age of stone temples is over.

What date were both of Israel's Temples destroyed? Why is this significant? _____

_____

Perhaps a third stone temple may be built someday in the future, but with the advent of the Messiah, a new era has begun. John the Baptist prophesied that Jesus would baptize us "with the Holy Spirit and fire." That prophecy came true on Pentecost. Forty years before the destruction of the Second Temple, the Lord initiated a new way that His Presence would dwell with us upon the Earth. No longer would the Presence of God dwell in a house of stone. Now He would dwell where He always intended to dwell since Adam and the creation of mankind. By the blood of Jesus, God now dwells within every believing heart.

No stone temple could ever compare with a Temple made by the hand of God Himself. Human beings were made in the image of God by the hand of God. And by His divine hand human beings were redeemed by the

Salvation of God through Christ Jesus. His new Temple on the Earth would not be made of stone and built by human beings. His Presence would now dwell in the most marvelous being He ever created—a creature so beautiful He stamped His own image on him, a creature so precious He personally stepped in to save him when an enemy corrupted him. This creature is you. Because you were designed and then redeemed by the Creator Himself, you are that Temple of which Haggai spoke.

In light of the biblical history to which new Temple was Haggai referring? _____

_____

You are the Temple whose "future glory is greater than its past glory." Do you see how utterly amazing you are, true believer? You are God's vision of the ultimate Temple in which to download His Presence. You are valuable to God and more significant to His plan in this age than you could possibly imagine.

What is the Spirit saying to you about how beautiful, amazing, and valuable you are? _____

_____

I leave you with the exhortation of the Prophet Haggai: "Be strong, be strong, be strong! And get to work. Do not be afraid. The Spirit of the Living God dwells within you." Become what you were born for. Become an earthen vessel filled with heaven's love and power. Become lightning in a bottle. Temple His Spirit!

How is the Lord calling you to live? _____

_____

Appendices

Appendix A

This is a sample of courses our church could offer for the Transformation Academy. Some already exist. Others are still being developed.

Transformation Academy
Comprehensive Course Catalog

A Message from Dr. Mike Palompo, D.Min.

The Heart of Transformation Academy
I am very excited to see not just the rebirth of our Transformation Academy but the new form it has taken. Since New Hope Central Oahu was born in 1999 we have journeyed a long way to realize that we will not be able to address all the critical issues of following Jesus in our Sunday morning services. So we inquired of the Lord, and He gave us a vision of the Temple. We were reminded that the ancient Temple was where God dwelt with His people (Exodus 25:8). Then the Lord connected the vision of the ancient Temple with a reality of truly epic proportions: WE are the Temple of His Holy Spirit (1 Corinthians 3:16; 6:29). God's Presence dwells within disciples of Christ. At NHCO our heart is to fully embrace the Manifest Presence of God in the Church. Our weekend services focus on salvation which is station one, the Bronze Altar. But there are six more stations beyond that. Our Transformation Academy uses the Temple as a template so we can temple His Spirit. So buckle your seatbelt, pilgrim! We're going on an odyssey to the deepest place of intimacy with God and the widest possible impact to the world.

Mission Statement
The mission of the Transformation Academy is to transform new

believers into reproductive disciples who temple the Holy Spirit.

THE OUTER COURT

I. Salvation (Station: Bronze Altar)
Transformation 100
WE BELIEVE that Salvation comes only by grace through faith in Jesus Christ.

Sunday AM Services: *Transformation 101*
Contemporary worship, dance, video, life-changing testimonies, and biblical, relevant messages all aimed at helping the unsaved find Jesus and newborn believers take the next step on the Road Map to Transformation. Commit yourself to attend every week and bring friends!

Grow with NHCO (Introduction Seminar to NHCO)
A brief seminar to introduce newcomers to NHCO's purpose, motto, core values, and Road Map to Transformation.

Bridge Events
Fun activities that introduce the community to NHCO and Christ (e.g., banquets, balls, sports)

II. Sanctification (Station: Bronze Basin)
Transformation 200
WE BELIEVE that Sanctification comes through the presence and power of the Holy Spirit.

Celebrate Recovery: *Transformation 201*
Through biblical teaching and support groups, Celebrate Recovery cooperates with the Spirit in setting individuals free from hurts, habits, and hang-ups. (Mondays, 7pm)

Pastor Lori Shimabukuro

Recognizing & Overcoming the Giants in Our Lives: *Transformation 203*
Instructor: Pastor Lori Shimabukuro
Wednesday Nights, 7-8:30 PM; Jun 10 – Jul 15, 2015 (6 weeks)

Synopsis: Each of us has giants in our lives. We will either surrender to them or overcome them: the outcome may be the difference between receiving or missing God's blessings. This class will help you to recognize the giants of fear, intimidation, depression, confusion or lack of faith and guide participants below the surface to see the roots of intimidation to discover: Why is it hard to say no? Why do I fear confrontation and avoid conflict? How do I identify intimidation and know how to break its hold? How does the fear of God help break feelings of intimidation? Insights will be provided to help grow in confidence and boldness and to walk in our own God-given authority. Study is based on 1 Samuel.

Course Outcomes:
Be the end of the course students will be able to:
- Recognize the giants of fear, intimidation, depression, confusion or lack of faith
- Understand the roots of intimidation to discover
- Break the hold of intimidation on one's life
- Understand how the fear of God helps break feelings of intimidation
- Gain insight on how to grow in confidence, boldness, and God-given authority

Myra and Cary Jones

Freedom & Authority Through Spiritual Transformation (FAST Class)
Transformation 210
DVD Instruction: Dr. Grant Mullen (http://drgrantmullen.com/)
Facilitators: Cary & Myra Jones
Thursday Nights: 7-9PM; Jun 4 – Jul 16, 2015 (7 weeks)

Synopsis: The series will focus on things that can prevent us from realizing our freedom—freedom from the penalty of sin (Jesus paid for it on the cross), no longer bound by the law (Jesus fulfilled it), and from exercising our authority—the power over the enemy (Christ is now with us and in us).

Course Outcomes:
By the end of the course will:
- Become aware of matters pertaining to the body, soul, and spirit
- Learn How these relate to our emotional well-being
- Understand how to address them in specific ways
- Walk in spiritual freedom and exercise our God-given authority
- Continue to be transformed into the image of Christ from glory to glory

Clean by Douglas Weiss, PhD: *Transformation 215*
Men's Small Group Study: A proven plan for men committed to

sexual integrity.

THE HOLY PLACE

III. Scripture (Station: Golden Table of Bread)
Transformation 300
WE BELIEVE that all Scripture is inspired by God and authoritative for life.

Ohana Group (Small Group): *Transformation 301*
The NHCO Ohana Group is a time of fun, friendship, and faith with a focus on discussing last Sunday's message and growing in God's Word.

Pastor Earl Morihara

How to Read the Bible with Understanding for Today
Transformation 310
Instructor: Pastor Earl Morihara
Thursday Nights, 6:30-8:30 PM; Jun 11 – Jul 30, 2015 (8 weeks)

Synopsis: This Study will assist participants in going beyond the discipline of Daily Devotional S.O.A.P Journaling as a means of understanding the bible, applying it to one's life and allowing the Holy Spirit to do the transformation. Guidelines to understand the various genres of which the bible is comprised will be examined. Various Bible Study Methods: Book Studies & Topical Studies (Examples include Character studies, where we study all the Bible says about particular person and Topical studies, where we study all the Bible says about a particular word or subject) will be introduced and practiced. Selected participants will share the facilitation role by becoming genre specialists to lead other participants in understanding that particular genre.

Required Text: *How to Read the Bible for All It's Worth*, Fee & Stuart

Course Outcome Objectives: Participants will . . .
1. Have a greater appreciation for God's Word, especially in doing Daily Devotions
2. Be able to read and understand *all* of God's Word with more confidence to make application for today and allow the Holy Spirit to do His transformational work
3. Be able to do various kinds of bible studies to grow in one's Christian life
4. Be more equipped to guide others to understand God's Word better
5. Grow more intimately with the "Living Word", Jesus Christ

IV. Testimony (Station: The Golden Lamp)
Transformation 400
WE BELIEVE that Christians are the light of the world.

DESIGN & DCAT Conference & Course: *Transformation 401*
DESIGN & DCAT assists believers discover, develop, and deploy their spiritual gifts for the purpose of Doing Church As Team. We may not all get to preach, but we can all testify.
(Textbook: *Doing Church As Team by Dr. Wayne Cordeiro*)

5-Fold Ministry Course: *Transformation 410*
Course based on: "So Christ himself gave the apostles, the prophets, the evangelists, the pastors and teachers, to equip his people for works of service, so that the body of Christ may be built

up" (Ephesians 4:11-12 NIV). Are you an apostle, prophet, evangelist, pastor, or teacher? Discover, develop, and deploy your five-fold ministry. (Textbook: *The Five Fingers of God* by Mark Tubbs)

Pastor Mark Palompo

Building & Leading Ministry Teams in 21st Century Churches
Transformation 450
Instructor: Pastor Mark Palompo
Wednesday Nights, 7:00-9:00 PM; Jun 10 – Jul 15, 2015 (6 weeks)

Synopsis: Re-thinking the way we build and lead teams towards effective ministry in the 21st Century Church. By the end of the course, students will be able to:
- Lead themselves in spiritual growth and think critically about overcoming challenges facing 21st Century leaders.
- Understand the Biblical basis of spiritual gifts and how to discover and lead from your spiritual gifts with maximum impact.
- Create and maintain culture in their respective areas of ministry that cause those they lead to flourish.
- Create leadership fractals that thrive and multiply.

V. Prayer (Station: Golden Altar of Incense)
Transformation 500
WE BELIEVE God's empowering presence comes through the

baptism of the Holy Spirit.

The Baptism of the Holy Spirit
Transformation 501
Scripture teaches that Jesus will "baptize you with the Holy Spirit and fire" (Matthew 3:11; Mark 1:8; Luke 3:16; Acts 1:5) and by the Spirit we will be "transformed from glory to glory" (2 Corinthians 3:18). This course will focus on the ministry of the Holy Spirit to transform us to deeper Christ-like character

Carol Miyashiro

Fruit Demonstrated and Gifts Activated – *Transformation 502*
Prerequisite Required: First take "The Baptism of the Holy Spirit: Transformation 501
Instructor: Carol Miyashiro
Meets on the 3rd Sunday of the month, 12:30-2:30 PM
Apr 12 – Aug 16

This course is geared for those newly baptized in the Holy Spirit and those who want to move in the gifts of the Spirit.
Content:
* Focus on the fruit of the Spirit as listed in Galatians 5:22-23
* Focus on the Gifts of the Spirit as listed in I Corinthians 12:7-11
* Focus on life of Jesus and the Apostles with fruit and gifts manifested

Practical assignments will be given and brief write up will be turned in at next month's class.

Prayer Tools Course: *Transformation 503*
This course equips you with practical tools for prayer in the Spirit.

The Holy Spirit: An Introduction: *Transformation 510*
Excellent video series on the Person of the Holy Spirit with John Bevere.

Awakening Conference: *Transformation 520*
This conference is designed to equip you with teaching on the Holy Spirit.

THE HOLY OF HOLIES

VI. Spiritual Leadership (Station: Ark of the Covenant)
Transformation 600
WE BELIEVE in the leading of the Holy Spirit.

Temple the Spirit Course: *Transformation 601*
A course on understanding God's design of the Temple as His way of taking us on an odyssey to *connect, equip,* and *transform,* in order to grow in intimacy with the Person and mission of Jesus and embrace how to *Temple the Spirit.*

God Things Course: *Transformation 602*
God Things contends for encounters with Jesus that first transform us Spiritually (y-axis) then the people around us (x-axis). In other words, there is a Spiritual transformation that takes place first in us that subsequently results in community transformation. The course focuses on the proper practice of biblical, Spiritual disciplines such solitude, silence, Sabbath keeping, and more.

Pastor Theresa Rosario

Life Skills for Leaders
Transformation 650
Instructor: Pastor Theresa Rosario
Wednesday Nights, 6-9 PM; June 3 – July 22, 2015 (8 weeks)
You will need your Campus Pastor's approval before taking this course.

Synopsis: A development course targeting 21st century church leaders for becoming God's speakers. It deals with grand principles in easy building blocks: upgrading character, personality, attitude, initiative, teamwork, and even how to become a great thinker.

Required Text: *Developing the Leader Within You,* John Maxwell

Course Outcomes:
By the end of the course, students will be able to:
• understand, articulate and apply biblical character traits for personal and ministerial leadership;
• understand key principals on attitude, initiative and inspiring teamwork;
• understand and apply important strategies for problem solving and conflict resolution through
Godly alliances;
• understand the difference between prophetic leadership and team based leadership and learning
when and how to walk in both;

• Have a good understanding of the Breadth of Trust diagram (The Leadership Scale) and
discovering where they are on the scale and continually evaluating where God wants them to be;
• How to become a great thinker

VII. Great Commission (Station: Mercy Seat)
WE BELIEVE the Holy Spirit empowers us to make disciples of all nations.

Multiply & RISE Course: *Transformation 701*
A study of the biblical basis for personal witnessing, including the central tenets of the Gospel; equips Christians in basic apologetics, establishing relationships with non-believers, and reproducing disciples who make disciples.

Men's RISE Retreat: *Transformation 702*
A retreat on equipping men for personal evangelism and making disciples who make disciples.

Hands of Hope: Outreach to the Poor: *Transformation 710*
The Hands of Hope Ministry is a partnership of several churches and organizations in the Central Oahu area. We offer hope to the homeless, poor and elderly with the love of Christ. Our hope is that our outward expression of care for these people will lead them to a new life and transformation through a relationship with Jesus Christ. We encourage and lead people to the one and only true hope...Jesus, while giving all glory to God.

Give Thanks Event: *Transformation 711*
Each year on Thanksgiving New Hope Central Oahu and concerned organizations of the community provide over 1,000 Thanksgiving meals in Jesus' name for Hawaii's homeless, less privileged, and disenfranchised. (Annually on Thanksgiving)

Marketplace Ministry: *Transformation 720*
The objective of this course is to equip you for effective evangelism and discipleship at school, work, and/or home.

Shema` Youth Ministry: *Transformation 730*
Equip parents to equip their children to Temple the Spirit and pass on the legacy of God's Manifest Presence from generation to generation.

New Hope Central Oahu also partners with these outstanding ministries:

Church on the Park: Worship Services for the Poor: *Transformation 735*
On the last Sunday of the month, Church on the Park provides outdoor Christian worship services on Hawaii's North Shore for those homeless, less privileged, and disenfranchised.

Ho'ōla Nā Pua: Ministry to Victims of Sex Trafficking: *Transformation 740*
Ho'ōla Nā Pua's (translation: "New Life for Our Children")
Our mission: to provide underage female victims of sex trafficking a holistic approach to mental and emotional healing in a long-term facility.

Village of Hope Uganda Mission: *Transformation 750*
The mission of Village of Hope Uganda is to provide a home, school, family, medical aid, counseling, skills training and—most importantly—God's love for formerly abducted children in Uganda.

Compassion International: *Transformation 755*
A church-based, child-focused, Christ-centered global ministry whose mission is to reach impoverished children for Christ by meeting their physical, emotional, and spiritual needs.

Appendix B

This is a sample personal inventory I created to help people discern which of the available classes in the summer catalog they should take. So it does not apply to every possible course in the comprehensive catalog.

Transformation Academy
Personal Inventory

Confused about which Transformation Academy class you should take this summer? Complete this brief personal inventory to find out.

Directions
Write the number that best describes you on your score sheet below. Add up your answers from left to right on your score sheet. Circle your highest score. Now you know which class to take!

5 = Strongly Agree   4 = Agree   3 = Neutral
2 = Disagree   1 = Strongly Disagree

1. I am not certain I will go to Heaven after I die.

2. I feel paralyzed by fear when faced with a challenging situation.

3. I struggle with shame.

4. I need to learn how to study the bible.

5. I need to learn how to build a ministry team.

6. I want to see more fruit of the Spirit in my life.

7. I aspire to be a ministry leader in the Church.

8. I do not feel I know Jesus in a personal way yet.

9. I experience feelings of intimidation and don't know why.

10. I do not feel that my emotions are under control.

11. I need to establish a daily devotion time to reflect on the Word.

12. I want to know what my spiritual gifts are.

13. I got baptized in the Spirit but don't know what to do next.

14. I have character flaws that prevent me from being a better Church leader.

15. The reason I go to Church is to show God I deserve to go to Heaven.

16. I lack confidence that I am someone who can serve God.

17. I clearly have anger management issues.

18. I do not know how to interpret the bible correctly.

19. I want to know how a ministry could be better led.

20. I see people operating in words of knowledge and wish I could do that.

21. I would like to become a more inspiring leader in the Church.

22. I believe in God but I'm not sure He is really there for me.

23. I wish I could become a more secure, confident person.

24. I see other Christians walk in authority and wish I could.

25. I want to learn how to teach others how to study the Bible.

26. I want my ministry to thrive, flourish, and multiply.

27. I want to learn how Jesus manifested both fruit and gifts in His life.

28. I would like to know how to become a great thinker.

SCORE SHEET
Transformation Academy
Personal Inventory

Directions. Add up your answers to the right. Circle your highest score(s). Analyze your results below. Sign up for your class!

Totals

1. _____	8. _____	15. _____	22. _____	A _____.
2. _____	9. _____	16. _____	23. _____	B _____.
3. _____	10. _____	17. _____	24. _____	C _____.
4. _____	11. _____	18. _____	25. _____	D _____.
5. _____	12. _____	19. _____	26. _____	E _____.
6. _____	13. _____	20. _____	27. _____	F _____.
7. _____	14. _____	21. _____	28. _____	G _____.

ANALYZE YOUR RESULTS
Transformation Academy
Personal Inventory

Based on your answers to the survey here is your best course of action. All sessions are held in the RISE Center.

If your highest score was "A"...
By coming to New Hope Central Oahu, you are about to go on the most important journey of your life—entering into an intimate relationship with God Himself! It is HUGE that you are coming to Church. We highly recommend that you commit yourself to coming to Church every weekend. If you have questions about the spiritual life, make an appointment with a campus pastor as soon as possible. He/She might even treat you to lunch!

If your highest score was "B"...
Sign up for "Recognizing and Overcoming the Giants in Our Lives" with Pastor Lori Shimabukuro.
Wednesday Nights, 7-8:30 PM; Jun 10 – Jul 15, 2015 (6 weeks)

If your highest score was "C"...
Sign up for "Freedom & Authority Through Spiritual Transformation (FAST Class)
Facilitators: Cary and Myra Jones
DVD Instruction with Dr. Grant Mullen
Thursday Nights: 7-9PM; Jun 4 – Jul 16, 2015 (7 weeks)

If your highest score was "D"...
Sign up for "How fo Read da Bible fo Understand Today"
Instructor: Pastor Earl Morihara
Thursday Nights, 6:30-8:30 PM; Jun 11 – Jul 30, 2015 (8 weeks)

If your highest score was "E"...

Sign up for "Building & Leading Ministry Teams in 21st Century Churches"
Instructor: Pastor Mark Palompo
Wednesday Nights, 7:00-9:00 PM
Jun 10 – Jul 15, 2015 (6 weeks)

If your highest score was "F"...

Sign up for "Fruit Demonstrated and Gifts Activated
Instructor: Carol Miyashiro
Meets on the third Sunday of the month, 12:30-2:30 PM
Apr 12 – Aug 16

If your highest score was "G"...

Sign up for "Life Skills for Leaders"
Instructor: Pastor Theresa Rosario
Wednesday Nights, 6-9 PM; June 3 – July 22, 2015 (8 weeks)

Prerequisite: You will need your Campus Pastor's approval before taking this course.

Now step out in faith, my friend, and sign up for a class! *Make* time to allow God to take you to your next level in your Spiritual transformation. You'll be glad you did. *Pastor Mike*

Appendix C

Shema` Family Discipleship

Church, classes and academies are important. They serve a vital purpose. But if we are to see the fulfillment of God's vision for us to temple His Spirit, something very dramatic needs to occur: a Spiritual Awakening of the Christian Family.

Most Christians have a favorite Bible verse. But did you know that in Israel everybody has the same favorite verse? Here it is:

Shema` Yisra'el 'Adonai 'eloheinu Adonai 'echad
Hear, O Israel! The Lord is our God, the Lord is one

Ve'ahavta 'et 'Adonai 'eloheikha
You shall love the Lord your God

Bekhol levavkha uvekhol nafshekha
With all your heart and with all your soul

Uvekhol me'odekha
And with all your might" (Deuteronomy 6:4 NASB).

What is the favorite bible verse of everyone in Israel? How would you summarize it? _____

_____

The title of this passage is derived from its first word, "shema`." Shema` is translated "hear," but it's really more like "listen up!" This is the theme verse of the people of Israel. Jews recite it when they first wake up in the morning. They repeat it before going to bed. Jewish moms tell it to their children like a bedtime story. And it is also the final prayer of one who is about to die.

From both a Jewish and Christian perspective the command to love God with all our being is the greatest commandment of all. Jesus affirms this in the synoptic Gospels. Don't forget Jesus was Jewish! So God's people everywhere must rediscover the power of the Shema`.

What does "Shema`" mean? _____

_____

It's simple to understand really. We have no other god but God. We worship no other. And we love God passionately with our whole being. Of all things in life, nothing matters more to us than God. If we are faithful to Him our lives will be blessed. The rains will come and our crops will grow. But disobey Him and go after other gods, and our lives will be cursed.

But the Shema` does not stop there. It not only tells us how to live, it also emphasizes how to pass this teaching on from generation to generation. This is very critical to catch.

Have you noticed how no matter where the Jews end up in the world, they never lose their identity as the people of God? Of all people groups they seem the most resistant to being assimilated by the cultures of the world. Do you know why that is? The reason is they have a powerful family life. And this comes from the Shema`.

The Shema` continues.

Vehayu haddevarim ha'elleh 'asher 'anokhi
These words which I am

metsavekha haiyom
commanding you today

`Al levavekha
Shall be on your heart

Veshinantam levanekha vedibarta bam
You shall diligently teach them to your children and shall talk of them

Beshivtekha beveytekha
When you sit down in your house

Uvlekhtekha badderekh
And when you walk by the way

Uvshokhbekha Uvkumekha
And when you lie down and when you rise up.

Uqshartam le'ot `al-yadekha
And bind them as a sign on your hand

Vehayu letotafot bein `eineykha
And they shall be as frontals on your forehead.

Ukhtavtam `al-mezuzot
And write them on the doorposts

Beytekha uvish`areykha
Of your house and on your gates
                        (Deuteronomy 6:5-9 NASB).

What does the Shema` say about teaching the next generation? _____

_____

God begins this section with an exhortation to parents: His commandment to love Him must be in our own hearts first. We will teach what we know but we will pass on who we are. God says to put His word in our heart. That means memorize it, meditate upon it, and above all live it.

Simultaneous with keeping His commandment is teaching it to the next generation. Notice the word *diligently*. The people of God must not be casual about training our children. We must be *diligent.* This requires thought, intentionality, and unceasing prayer.

God is even specific about when and where to disciple our kids: as we sit in our house, as we walk along the way, before we go to sleep, and first thing as we wake up. The Church can help, but this is obviously talking about the family life of God's people.

What clues do you find that God is very serious about the parents' role in training children? _____

_____

Who is ultimately responsible for the training of children? That's right. Parents.

Parents must not abdicate the raising of their children to anyone or anything else. Do not leave this urgent matter to a youth ministry or a Sunday School. For God's sake do not leave this in the hands of public education or the government! No one has greater authority over children than their parents.

Dad and mom, God gave the responsibility to disciple your children in Christ primarily to you.

Do not surrender this role to anybody else.

How is this related to *Lightning in a Bottle* and our odyssey to temple the Holy Spirit? This gives us a vision for the goal of our parenting.

What is your goal as a parent? That your child become a good citizen? A difference maker in society? A doctor? Lawyer? Engineer? Some of us might settle for "make enough money so you can move out of the house and support yourself!" While others might say, "Just stay out of jail."

The real question we must ask is, "Lord, what is *Your* goal for our children?" Why did God bring our children into this world? For what purpose were they created? Now, that is the million dollar question right there. Our children were created by God to know Him intimately— to temple His Spirit! And the family is the primary setting where they will learn and experience this reality.

What is God's vision for our children? _____

_____

This means that parents must learn the Temple Template first.

Recall that the Shema` says to teach the children while you sit at home, as you walk along the way, before you go to sleep, and first thing as you wake up. The Church youth ministry cannot do those things! That's a job for godly, Spirit-led parents.

What is the role of the Church youth ministry in raising kids? _____

_____

Did you note the four settings where we disciple our children? As we sit in our house, when we walk along the way, as we wake up, and before we go to bed. There is no mention of classes and youth meetings.

As we "sit in our house" means as we hang out together at home, we have heart-to-heart conversations with our kids about God. Dinner time is a wonderful time for this to happen. The TV should be off and no electronic devices allowed at the table. Instead, it's time to have an informal Q & A about God, life, and the Bible. It's time to share testimony on any God Things that happened that day. Our family found it challenging to all sit together at breakfast and lunch, so we made it a point to have dinner together as a family. Remember, no electronic devices allowed at the table; have a conversation with one another.

Another time is when we "walk along the way." This means as you're driving to school, going to the store, running errands, or on your way to soccer practice have a conversation with your kids about God. Again, it might mean turning off the radio and putting away electronic devices. Obviously, it's not every single time you're in the car. But do take advantage of any "teachable moment" the Holy Spirit provides you as your kid is "stuck" there sitting next to you.

Then the Shema` says talk about God "when you lie down." One of the best times to speak with our children is when we tuck them in at bedtime. Mona and I found this was an especially wonderful moment. For one the kids don't want to go to sleep! So you can read to them, pray over them, anoint them, bless them, and talk all you want.

Finally, the Shema` says to interact with our children when we "rise up." First thing in the morning have a mini devotion time at breakfast. Pray over your children before they go to school. This will help them grow in their awareness of God's Presence with them throughout the day.

Don't you love how specific the Shema` is? God spells out the precise moments parents look for opportunities to speak into the lives of their children—as you sit in your house, as you walk along the way, as you lie down, and as you rise up. Very practical! This is God's vision for how to train up a child in how they should live—discipleship in everyday life.

You may have noticed that Jewish homes put something called a mezuzah on the right doorpost of their home about one-third of the way down from the top. I have one of those on my house. What is this? Actually, the word mezuzah means "doorpost," but the thing the Shema` is referring to is a small container, like a little cubby hole. Inside it is a miniature copy of the Shema`.

God is so intensely adamant that we never forget this command that He wants it displayed on the doorpost of our homes. Each time a Jew enters or exits his home he places his hand over the mezuzah and prays to remind himself, "Listen up! Today, God loves you and you walk in His amazing Presence. Be sure to love Him with your whole being, through every thought, word, and action."

This is reminiscent of when the ancient Hebrews marked their doorposts with lamb's blood during Passover. Today the doorposts of our hearts are marked by the blood of Jesus.

God also commanded us to put reminders on our foreheads and on our hands. How crazy is that! Do you see how incredibly insistent God is that we follow Him and mentor our children to follow Him? The Shema` is AWESOME!

How can you tell that God is really insistent that parents mentor their children? _____

_____

Before I became a pastor I was a youth minister for 16 years. I would lead kids to Jesus and disciple them best I could. But I only had them for four years max. Then they would graduate from high school and I wouldn't see them as much. Sometimes their graduation day was the last time I ever saw them.

One day I remember feeling real frustrated by that. I told the Lord, "There is so much to teach these kids! I can't do it in the 90 minutes I have with them in youth group. What these kids need is someone who will be with them 24 hours a day!" It was as if the Lord said to me, "I already thought of that. They're called parents."

When I first started youth ministry I was single. But during that time I had gotten married and became a parent. Your perspective changes dramatically once you have kids!

At New Hope Central Oahu we don't have a conventional youth ministry led by a youth pastor (with cool clothes, a hip hairstyle, sings like a pop star, and plays guitar). Our youth ministry is led by parents.

Our vision is to train parents to mentor their own children and help other parents mentor theirs.

We're not opposed to having cool youth leaders help out. The leadership of our youth is made up of (1) Parents, (2) Partners (which includes the cool youth guy), (3) Peers (student leaders), and (4) Pastors. But our primary focus is on training parents to fulfill their God-given role to disciple their youth.

We are praying for Shema` Family Discipleship to become a vision that will catch on with more and more parents in society. It is God's original design for how to help the next generation temple the Spirit. He wants generation after generation to be lightning in a bottle!

What is Shema` Family Discipleship and what part is the Lord calling you to play in that? _____

_____

By faith what did the Holy Spirit say to you in this section? How will you obey Him? _____

_____

About the Author

Michael M. Palompo is the founder and senior pastor of New Hope Central Oahu on the island of Oahu, Hawaii established on Easter Sunday, April 4, 1999. NHCO was historically the first of many church plants from New Hope Oahu under Pastor Wayne Cordeiro. Mike is a proud graduate of the Radford High School Bicentennial Class of 1976 where he was student council president. He has a BA in Psychology from California State University – San Francisco, where he was a member of Phi Beta Kappa and graduated summa cum laude. He has a Master of Christian Studies degree from Regent College in Vancouver, BC, (where he studied under Eugene Peterson, J.I. Packer, and Gordon Fee). And he has a Doctor of Ministry degree in *Spiritual Transformation* from The King's University in Los Angeles, where he studied under Chancellor Jack Hayford.

Mike published his first book in 2011, *God Things: Encounters with Jesus That Transform Us* (available on Amazon). He is an adjunct professor at Pacific Rim Christian University (formerly New Hope Christian College) in Honolulu, HI where he has been teaching Spiritual Transformation, Evangelism, and Discipleship since it was established in 1998. His book elaborates on his passion for the Manifest Presence and personal intimacy with God. It is also the textbook for his course.

Mike has lived in Mililani, HI since 1991 with his lovely wife, Mona (married 1983), daughter Rachael (born 1989), and youngest son, Caleb (born 1998). Eldest son, Mark (born 1986), is married to Jalee (since 2012).

www.newhopecentraloahu.org

(l to r) Caleb, Mike, Mona, Rachael, Jalee, and Mark

Acknowledgements

Beyond what words can express and with all my heart, I thank the following:

The staff of New Hope Central Oahu, Earl Morihara and Mark Palompo (Mililani Campus), Lori Shimabukuro (Wahiawa Campus), Glenn and Theresa Rosario (Haleiwa Campus), Andrell Aoki, Pam Chun, and Jane Amano, for being our Dream Team, whose Spiritual leadership and great humility paved the way for the birth of a Church culture focused on God's Manifest Presence.

Our Church board members, Dave Alvarico, Rich Fewell, Roy Helepololei, Les Lichtenberg, Will Lu, and Brian Misaka, whose servant leadership embraced the vision of a Church "anchored to God's Word and led by His Spirit."

The people of New Hope Central Oahu, fertile soil, and willing to follow Jesus on a great adventure that's both scary and exciting.

Pastor Wayne Cordeiro, mentor, friend, and Spiritual father of our New Hope ohana.

Mark Olmos, we couldn't have imagined at our conversion in 1975 how amazing a quest it would be to follow Jesus.

Yamit McCormick, friend and colleague, who taught me Yeshua's language and culture. Baruch Hashem!

My parents, Diosdado and Angelina Palompo, my sister, Leila Fregoso and her family, my brothers, Jay, Ray, and

Joe, and their families, and our whole clan—Asercions, Fregosos, Ignacios, Moores, Palompos, Sagerts, and Vus. My first companions on our journey with Jesus.

My precious children, Mark and Jalee, Rachael, and Caleb, there is no father's blessing I would withhold from you.

Mona, my love for a lifetime whose spirit upholds me in Jesus like no other human being on Earth.

Jesus, Savior, Lord, Messiah, Immanuel, Master, Transformer, Rabbi, High Priest, and King, whose Spirit fills my *Mishkan* Temple for His glory.

45051780R00155

Made in the USA
Charleston, SC
11 August 2015